# A BETTER CHOICE:
## THE MANAGER'S GUIDE TO SKILLS-FIRST HIRING

# A BETTER CHOICE:

## *THE MANAGER'S GUIDE TO SKILLS-FIRST HIRING*

by

Mark A. Smith, Ph.D.

Smith Bros

A Better Choice: The Manager's Guide to Skills-First Hiring
First Edition

Copyright © 2024 by Mark A. Smith

ISBN number: 9798882533112

**Author's Note:**
No part of this publication may be reproduced, stored in a retrieval system, or transmitted in any form or by any means, electronic, mechanical, photocopying, recording, scanning, or otherwise, without the prior written permission of the author. You can reach the author at msmitty63633@outlook.com.

This publication is designed to provide accurate and authoritative information regarding the subject matter covered. It is sold with the understanding that the author is not engaged in rendering legal, investment, accounting, or other professional services. While the author has used his best efforts in preparing this book, he makes no representations or warranties concerning the accuracy or completeness of the contents of this book and specifically disclaims any implied warranties of merchantability or fitness for a particular purpose. No warranty may be created or extended by sales representatives or written sales materials. The advice and strategies contained herein may not be suitable for your situation. You should consult with a professional when appropriate. The author shall not be liable for any loss of profit or any other commercial damages, including but not limited to special, incidental, consequential, personal, or other damages.

You can find Mark on LinkedIn at: linkedin.com/in/mark-smith-ph-d-1776201a8.
You can also email him directly at: msmitty63633@outlook.com.

## Dedication

To my loving family, who have supported me every step of the way. And specifically for my lovely wife, Kira, my reviewer and consistent source of encouragement and inspiration.

Thanks also to Jon Canger and team at Zennia Research for helpful comments in earlier drafts of the book.

I would also like to thank our friends at Arthur Murray Dance Studio in Alexandria, VA, and Virginia Ballet Company in Burke, VA, who helped me get my mind off this book during my break times.

# TABLE OF CONTENTS

# EARLY REVIEWS

*"A Better Choice" offers a refreshing perspective on hiring. Its focus on skills-first hiring has revolutionized the way I am thinking about talent acquisition. It's a must-read for any manager looking to create high-performing teams.*

- Kimberly Vargas, HR director at the San Diego Symphony

*Having dealt with a multitude of unreliable systems for hiring talent, I was intrigued by the concept of skills-first hiring introduced in "A Better Choice." The practical tips and actionable insights by Dr. Smith are instrumental in reshaping our hiring strategy. I wholeheartedly endorse this book to all hiring managers.*

- Shaun Willis, partner and founder at Willis Law

*There is a LOT of great stuff in this book, and any hiring manager would learn a tremendous amount about the hiring process from reading it.*

- Jon Canger, former HR executive

*"A Better Choice" is more than just a book; it's a blueprint for success in hiring. Its insights into skills-based hiring made me fundamentally rethink my old recruitment strategy. I highly recommend it to any manager looking to find top talent.*

- Frank Zappia, business owner – Zappia Vending (retired)

2

*The secret of my success is
that we have gone to
exceptional lengths to hire
the best people in the world.*

Steve Jobs

# CHAPTER 1

# SETTING THE STAGE: THE IMPORTANCE OF HIRING RIGHT

**What the Hiring Manager Needs to Remember**

Effective hiring is essential for any organization, and hiring managers are usually responsible for making the final decision about whom to hire. However in most larger companies, managers are often not involved in much of the hiring process. This division of labor can be advantageous, as talent acquisition professionals take care of many of the mundane tasks in the process. However, as the hiring manager, you need to be aware of the process your company uses and ask the right questions to ensure that you are equipped to find the best candidates for your open roles.

The success of any organization is determined by the quality of its employees and leaders. Even companies with great products and endless markets can be harmed beyond repair by the poor decisions and performance of individuals. Further, the people who work for you define your corporate culture, so changing employees can affect the culture for better or worse. Therefore, it is terribly important for companies to hire the best people who have the right skills, competencies, and the highest potential to succeed.

But in the current employment landscape, relying on standard metrics like college degrees and the number of years of experience as the main measures of *job qualification* has become outdated. It's time to prioritize a **skills-first** approach to hiring, which values an individual's ability to perform the job above all else. For too long, people have believed that the *only* way to gain valuable skills needed to find good jobs is through a college degree. However, this assumption ignores the many alternative pathways and learning opportunities available to individuals outside of the traditional academic system.

Countless talented individuals possess immense creativity and drive but may not have had the time, means, or desire to pursue a college education. By prioritizing skills over degrees, we open the doors of opportunity to these individuals, tapping into a pool of talent that has long been overlooked.

We have methods of measuring and evaluating job-related skills that can effectively replace the previous emphasis on using college degrees to screen job applicants. Focusing on skills allows us to break down barriers to entry and promote greater diversity and inclusivity within our organizations. By recognizing and valuing the diverse ways in which individuals acquire skills, whether through self-directed learning, vocational training, apprenticeships, or other non-traditional means, we create a more equitable playing field where everyone has the chance to succeed based on their abilities rather than their credentials.

The rapid pace of technological change means that the competencies needed in today's workforce are constantly evolving. Relying solely on outdated notions of qualification based on degrees not only limits our talent pool but also hinders our ability to adapt and innovate in an ever-changing environment.

By shifting to skills-first hiring practices, we empower individuals to reach their full potential regardless of their educational background. This approach also positions organizations for success in the dynamic and competitive landscape of the 21st century. It's time to level the playing field, foster diversity, and propel our organizations forward into a future where meritocracy reigns supreme.

## THE ROLE OF THE HIRING MANAGER

As a hiring manager, it is your responsibility to hire the right people for your organization. Although talent acquisition professionals and hiring processes can be helpful, the final hiring decision usually rests with you. And if you make poor hires, company leadership will likely ask you why mistakes were made. In this book, I will outline a standard hiring process that prioritizes a skills-first approach. This method ensures that you consider candidates from diverse backgrounds and carefully evaluate everyone's *true* qualifications for the role.

In addition to knowledge and skills, it is also crucial to assess a candidate's cultural fit for your organization during the hiring process. To achieve long-term organizational success and employee engagement, you must prioritize alignment with your organization's values, goals, and work culture at the hiring stage. As a result, I recommend using tests and assessments that focus on both skills and fit with the company. I also recommend using planned questions during the interview phase that evaluate both technical abilities and cultural compatibility. This approach can identify candidates with the necessary skills and alignment with your organization's culture, contributing positively to the team dynamic.

---

Instead of only considering candidates with college degrees, many jobs can be filled by assessing candidates for technical and soft skills.

---

In fact, your hiring decisions might be THE most important decisions that you will make as a manager. Indeed, it would help if you remembered that a new hire making a $75,000 salary is (in many cases) a $1,000,000 hire, given the total cost of compensation and benefits over a ten-year tenure. This is a huge investment for any organization to make, and it needs to be an effective use of resources.

Here is another way of looking at the situation. Even if you have world-class people management practices – from total compensation and performance management to training and recognition – the talent that you bring in sets the <u>upper limit</u> on what your team or company can achieve. While a basketball team of the tallest and most athletic players may not win *all* their games, most of us would bet on them having more wins than a team of short, unathletic, unskilled players. I would even make the same bet if the second team had a much better coach.

I have also talked with managers about how wrong hiring decisions can hurt their job performance as a manager. This is in addition to the bad hires not reaching their desired job performance levels. Making the wrong hires tends to require a large amount of your management time. You must monitor them more closely, spend more time coaching them, and fix their mistakes. And this does not factor in the negative impact they may have on other team members. It is hard for you to do your job as a manager if you need to spend time doing the jobs of your team members.

## OVERVIEW OF THIS BOOK

In this book, I will provide a comprehensive overview of the various stages involved in the hiring process and will also highlight the typical responsibilities of a hiring manager. While certain aspects of the hiring process are primarily managed by the Human Resources (HR) department and the talent acquisition team in larger companies, certain other aspects rely heavily on the hiring manager's involvement.

Here is the funnel graphic which shows a common hiring process in today's organizations.

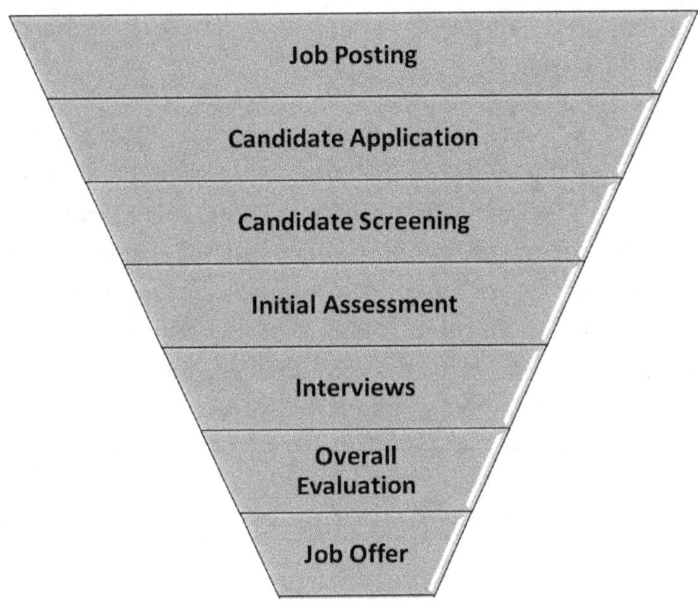


I understand that many hiring managers work in small organizations that do not have a dedicated talent acquisition professional or recruiting team. In such cases, the hiring manager is responsible for everything, although some parts of the hiring process may be shortened or skipped in small companies. For instance, I know that most small companies do not use tests and assessments to help evaluate candidates. However, it is still important for the hiring manager to understand the steps of a typical hiring process, so they know the options for the hiring process. And even if there is a recruiter to help with such tasks as reviewing initial candidate resumes, the hiring manager should still understand the options for resume review and how to do so consistently to ensure fairness across candidates.

Moreover, some organizations have their own prescribed hiring process that differs from the typical process we will be discussing. Unionized or governmental organizations, for example, may follow their own process. However, they still must go through a series of steps to find the best candidate from a larger pool of applicants.

Throughout the rest of this book, I will cover the steps of a typical hiring process. However, in this early summary, I would like to highlight two key parts that are particularly relevant for hiring managers: 1) assessing key job skills and 2) making a final hiring decision.

## USING ASSESSMENTS TO ENSURE CANDIDATES HAVE THE KEY SKILLS

In a skills-first hiring approach, tests and assessments are integral for ensuring that a high-quality candidate gets the job. This is true because these assessments often take on the role of evaluating if applicants have high enough skills and abilities. In the old model of hiring, companies used educational credentials to evaluate the level of knowledge and competence of applicants. However, many organizations (especially smaller ones) have not used any assessments to check the competencies of individuals.

> In skills-first hiring, proper use of valid assessments is the key to ensuring that you make good hires.

Finding the right assessments starts early in the hiring process when you identify the key skills and competencies required for success in the job. This process takes various steps, including a job analysis. Once identified, these skills should be listed in the job description to attract job applicants with the right skills.

However, it is during an official assessment step that the hiring process becomes more serious and rigorous. These assessments can be used to ensure that you understand both technical and soft skill levels before determining which applicants move forward in your hiring process. Keep in mind that although these skills are identified as part of the hiring process, assessments are neither foolproof nor 100% accurate. And the validity of assessments should not be blindly believed. Hiring managers and HR professionals should ask good questions to the test owners or internal testing experts about how to appropriately use assessments and interpret their results. It is important to take the use of assessments seriously, while also questioning certain aspects and looking for evidence of why the assessment is relevant for the role.

In the book, we will discuss the balance between taking the assessments seriously with skeptically questioning the results. We will also review the different ways of ensuring that tests and assessments are valid. It is important to emphasize that test validity cannot be assumed and should be demonstrated through test validation evidence.

MAKING A FINAL HIRING DECISION AMONG THE FINAL CANDIDATES

Once the entire hiring process is completed, and many applicants have been narrowed down to just a few, the final hiring decision must be made. Typically, the hiring manager is solely responsible for this final decision, and there are usually no rules to determine which final candidate should receive the job offer. Many managers simply rely on their feelings and general judgment at this point, which can lead to a variety of problems down the road. However, there is a better way. There are best practices that hiring managers should follow to make the best decision. And if they are unsure which candidate is best, there are steps to take to clarify the best hiring decision.

In Chapter 7, we will review the process for hiring managers to make their final decision in much more detail later in this book.


## WHY HAVE I WRITTEN THIS BOOK?

As someone with a background in organizational psychology and who has worked in HR consulting and with the Society for Human Resource Management, I have seen the reality of hiring and assessment for many companies. Over the years, I have seen both good and bad hiring practices. In larger organizations, HR professionals are usually responsible for the hiring process, but hiring managers play important roles in some parts of the process.

However, I have also observed that hiring managers usually have limited knowledge about the entire hiring process. This lack of broad understanding can lead to important hiring mistakes. My goal with this book is to enlighten you on the overall hiring process so that you can be more effective in your role as a hiring manager.

As an unbiased expert in the hiring process, my goal is to help you understand the reality of the hiring process and the mistakes that companies often make. For instance, research has shown that providing potential job applicants with an honest and realistic job preview leads to better and more successful employees[1]. Honest job previews (including the negative parts of the job) can help employees stay longer and trust their organizations more. However, many hiring managers refuse to reveal negative aspects of their company during the hiring process. While this thought process is understandable, it can lead to increased turnover and worse hires over time.

In this book, I will also share my understanding of applicant assessments and tests. I will offer some perspectives that may be controversial, but you should know them. In particular, having worked in the testing industry, I have seen that *many current applicant screening assessments do not have evidence that they work as claimed.*

This is not to say that assessments are completely useless, but they have not *demonstrated* their usefulness for specific jobs and organizations. Therefore, as a hiring manager and consumer of assessments, I strongly advise that you ask for evidence of their effectiveness before using them. **Good assessments should have evidence of validity.** This is in line with the scientific process, which requires proof of effectiveness before any intervention can be deemed effective. I will discuss what kind of proof you should ask for later in the book, including the idea of test validity and the types of evidence that can demonstrate the usefulness of an assessment.

## AUDIENCE FOR THIS BOOK

Hiring is a crucial process for any organization, and it is usually viewed as an HR issue. However, *I did not write this book for HR professionals.* Instead, it is addressed to hiring managers and intended to help them understand the hiring process. Therefore, I am going to talk with <u>you</u> – the hiring manager – for the rest of the book.

Talent acquisition should not be a "black box" where decisions are made behind closed doors. Instead, it should be an open and transparent process where everyone understands the steps and decision-making process.

FOR MORE INFORMATION

1.  Breaugh, J. A. (2009). The Use of Realistic Job Previews in the Study of Applicant Decision Making and Employee Attitudes and Behavior: A Review. *Journal of Applied Psychology, 94*(4), 859–873.

11

*It's time we stop making the assumption that the only place to get skills is through college and getting a college degree.*

Mark Smith (author)

# CHAPTER 2

# UNDERSTANDING THE SKILLS-FIRST HIRING APPROACH

- What Is a Skills-First Hiring Approach?

- Benefits of Prioritizing Skills Over Traditional Credentials

- Common Misconceptions and Challenges of a Skills-First Approach

---

**What the Hiring Manager Needs to Remember**

Many companies are shifting away from traditional screening methods, such as only considering candidates with education degrees and a specific number of years of experience. Instead, they are adopting a skills-first hiring approach, which emphasizes the skills and competencies of applicants. Rather than assuming that a degree or work experience equates to competence, these organizations are identifying and measuring the skills and other traits of candidates directly. This enables them to consider a wider range of job applicants and select the most qualified candidate for the job. As a hiring manager, it is important to be open to this approach and to embrace a broader definition of what it means to be qualified for a job.

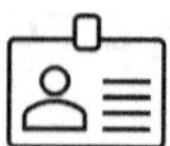

Welcome to the era of skills-first hiring! In today's job market, the old ways of hiring are making way for a new approach that puts skills and competencies front and center. Gone are the days when a college degree was the golden ticket to a good job. Many qualified candidates were unfairly overlooked just because they didn't finish their degrees. But times are changing. Companies are waking up to the fact that what truly matters are the skills and abilities a candidate brings to the table. Instead of fixating on diplomas or degrees, they are zeroing in on the specific competencies needed for each role, whether technical or soft skills.

Indeed, a 2017 study from Harvard Business School found that over 60 percent of companies have turned down applicants with the right skills and experience because lacked a college degree[1]. However, more recent data shows that companies are asking for degrees less often. This is not to say that skills-first hiring has completely caught on, but I believe this is the beginning of an important trend.

In this chapter, we'll delve into the concept of skills-first hiring and explore why it should be the go-to strategy for forward-thinking companies.

## SKILLS-FIRST HIRING

Unlike the conventional focus of evaluating job applicants which starts with education level and years of experience, skills-first hiring prioritizes a candidate's demonstrated skills and competencies. It does not matter if they acquired these skills from universities or YouTube. In some cases, these can be demonstrated by certifications and other alternative credentials. In other cases, applicants demonstrate their skills via computer-based assessments or in a structured interview process. In recent years, I have worked with large organizations that are just starting to see the benefits of a focus on assessing applicant skills, rather than screening based on traditional degrees.

But I should also acknowledge important information right from the start. College degrees are still necessary for some jobs. This is the case for many advanced degrees and degrees that effectively demonstrate skills that can be acquired (almost) exclusively in the college/university system. However, *many jobs do not require the knowledge and skills that are taught in college*. These are the jobs that are changing in a skills-first environment.

This new focus on skills and competencies allows a more inclusive and effective approach to talent acquisition. This shift also brings other benefits for organizations that are willing to embrace it. For instance, companies like Google have utilized the idea of skills-first hiring, relying more on skill assessments and other methods to identify candidates with the competencies to fit with the company's direction and culture.

In my experience, hiring managers are often reluctant to change the hiring process in this way. They commonly comment that they do not want to "water down" the process or eliminate important opportunities for candidate screening that they have used for years. While this concern is understandable, I maintain that making these changes to the hiring process will improve the process. It will <u>not</u> create a situation where worse candidates are hired. As long as companies use skill assessments and/or alternative credentials to evaluate candidates, organizations will be able to fill their jobs with quality workers. Simply put, *we do not need to continue assuming that colleges are the only place to acquire skills needed for good jobs*.

Even though many companies have started to use a skills-first approach when posting job openings, the hiring outcomes have not changed much to this point. For example, a 2024 study by the Burning Glass Institute showed that the vast majority of new hires in roles where a college requirement was eliminated still had college degrees[2]. In other words, the hiring rules have changed, but the hiring outcomes have remained the same. These results demonstrate that the skills-first approach still has a ways to go. However, in my view, the key is eliminating the *barriers* for job applicants; seeing different hiring outcomes will likely take place over the course of time.

## What's Wrong with Hiring Based on Traditional Degrees?

First of all, I should state that I am not opposed to traditional universities. After all, I spent ten great years of my life at Hope College and the University of South Florida. In many cases, colleges provide qualilty education for students and allow them the opportunity to develop skills that are needed for their eventual jobs. However, most colleges and universities are terribly inefficient in teaching job-related skills. If you think of a traditional four-year bachelor's degree, most students spend about two years taking classes that provide them with relevant skills. If someone is studying software engineering, should a company care that they also learned about English literature?

And they are not just inefficient in terms of time spent finishing a degree. They are also very expensive – particularly in the United States. It is quite common for students to accumulate $100,000 or more in student loans during their college years. Why force your job candidates to go through this process when you only care about what they learned in a relatively small number of classes?

> Universities are still a viable place to find careers and develop skills, but they are not the only place.

It is also clear that many students use their time in college to explore and find a career that fits them. Indeed, colleges and universities are places where students find their passions and accumulate a wide variety of skills. But they are not the *only* places. As a society, we should be able to look past college degrees to find ways to understand the skills and competencies of each person as it relates to their potential success in different jobs.

## AN EXPANDED DEFINITION OF BEING QUALIFIED FOR THE JOB

As I advocate for a different approach to evaluating job candidates, it is also a good time to reconsider the notion of what it truly means to be "qualified" for a job. The traditional definition of "most qualified" has been based on the person with the highest credentials, usually in terms of documented education and years of experience. For instance, a candidate with a Master's degree would have been considered the most qualified compared to those with only a bachelor's degree. Similarly, a candidate with seven years of related experience would be more qualified than another candidate with four years of experience. Although this definition is straightforward and easy to assess when evaluating job applicants, I believe it is flawed and over-simplified. Therefore, I suggest a new definition of what it truly means to be the most qualified candidate for a job.

> Being the "most qualified" for a job means that the person is the one who **is most likely to succeed and thrive in the role** – both in the short and long term.

Expanding the definition of being "qualified" for a job to encompass the idea of being the most likely to succeed and thrive in the role, both in the near and long term, offers several compelling advantages:

1. *Focus on Potential and Fit*: Traditional qualifications often prioritize past role tenure and degrees, which do not fully capture an individual's potential or suitability for a role. By emphasizing the likelihood of success and thriving in the role, this expanded definition should encourage you to consider more factors. This includes cultural fit, personality traits, and growth potential. This will lead to better alignment between candidates and job requirements.

2. *Adaptability to Changing Roles*: In today's rapidly changing job market, the skills and competencies required for success in many jobs are constantly evolving. Rigid adherence to traditional qualifications may limit the pool of candidates and overlook individuals who possess the ability to adapt, learn quickly, and excel in dynamic environments. Expanding the definition of job qualification allows for greater flexibility in assessing candidates based on their ability to find success in evolving roles and industries.

3. *Promotion of Diversity and Inclusion*: Traditional qualifications can inadvertently continue biases and barriers to entry for individuals from underrepresented groups or non-traditional backgrounds. By shifting the focus to potential and likelihood of success, organizations can create more inclusive hiring processes that recognize and value diverse perspectives, experiences, and talents. This not only fosters a more equitable playing field but can also enhance innovation and creativity as people with different backgrounds are being placed in new roles.

4. *Long-Term Performance and Retention*: Hiring individuals who are not only technically proficient but also well-suited to the role in terms of personality, values, and motivations can lead to greater job satisfaction,

performance, and retention over time. Employees who feel aligned with their roles and the organizational culture are more likely to be engaged, committed, and productive over time, contributing to overall organizational success.

5. *Holistic Evaluation of Candidates*: Expanding the definition of job qualification encourages a more holistic evaluation of candidates, considering a broader range of factors beyond traditional credentials. This includes assessing soft skills, such as communication, teamwork, and general problem-solving, as well as considering candidates' potential for growth, adaptability, and cultural fit. By considering the full spectrum of candidate attributes, organizations can make more informed hiring decisions that lead to better outcomes for individuals as well as entire organizations.

## POTENTIAL BENEFITS OF PRIORITIZING SKILLS OVER TRADITIONAL CREDENTIALS

### EXPANDED TALENT POOL

Using a skills-first hiring approach can help organizations discover candidates who would have been overlooked in a traditional hiring process. Eliminating unnecessary job requirements can significantly expand the talent pool, leading to an increase in the number of initially qualified candidates. This change can help fill roles that were previously difficult to fill with candidates who are not only suitable for the job but also hold potential for future positions within the organization. As many companies encounter challenges in filling positions, adopting a skills-first approach is a great way to address this issue.

### TALENT POOL DIVERSITY

Organizations can also expand the *types* of applicants that they get by prioritizing skills over traditional qualifications. This approach allows them to be more inclusive in their recruitment process by considering candidates from non-traditional backgrounds. This includes those who have changed careers, self-taught professionals, military veterans, and individuals from underrepresented groups. For instance, IBM's New Collar Initiative prioritizes skill sets over degrees, and they found that it has led to greater diversity in their company[3].

## IMPROVED JOB FIT AND PERFORMANCE

Organizations can also benefit from skills-first hiring by matching candidates more accurately with job requirements. This can lead to better job fit and performance. By assessing candidates based on their specific skills and competencies that are relevant to the role, you can identify individuals who are better suited to succeed in the position. As an example, Google is known for its use of skills-first hiring, which includes assessments and behavioral interviews to identify candidates with the necessary skills and cultural fit for the company[5].

## FASTER TIME-TO-HIRE

Focusing on the skills and competencies that can be demonstrated by the candidates can help speed up the hiring process by simplifying the evaluation and selection process. Instead of waiting for a perfect candidate with specific traditional qualifications, companies can more quickly identify good candidates based on their demonstrated skills. Consequently, the time required to hire the right candidate can be reduced, enabling companies to fill critical roles more efficiently and effectively.

## EMPLOYEE ENGAGEMENT AND RETENTION

Employees who are hired based on their skills might be more satisfied and engaged in their jobs, which in turn could lead to higher retention rates. When individuals are placed in roles where they can fully utilize their strengths and abilities, they become more motivated to contribute to the success of the company. This alignment between job requirements and employee skills can foster a positive work environment and enhance job satisfaction. For instance, Airbnb has a culture that values employee contributions and focuses on promoting and hiring based on skills[5]. They report that this focus helps to create a culture of engagement and retention.

## FUTURE-PROOF THE WORKFORCE

Skills-based hiring reduces the importance of traditional education degrees and prioritizes skills that can be changed more easily. It enables organizations to build a workforce that is adaptable and resilient in the face of technological advancements and industry changes. It also does not rely on universities to keep up with the times. This approach helps future-proof the talent pipeline and ensures that employees have new skills and the capacity to evolve with business needs. Amazon's Career Choice program is an example of how organizations can provide employees with opportunities to develop new skills and pursue career paths within and outside the company[6]. This program moves the focus from traditional education to demonstrated skills. It empowers employees to learn skills outside of the university system and thrive in a changing work landscape.

## BIPARTISAN POLITICAL ISSUE

In the summer of 2023, I was invited to serve as an expert witness for the U.S. House Committee on Education and the Workforce. The hearing was entitled "Competencies Over Degrees: Transitioning to a Skills-Based Economy." During the session, we heard reports from other experts and answered questions from both Republican and Democratic representatives who were almost entirely supportive of this issue. Both sides of the political divide in the United States agree that companies should place less emphasis on traditional educational degrees when evaluating job candidates. After the hearing, I was told by Congressional staffers that such bipartisanship is exceedingly rare. To learn more about this hearing, please refer to an article in Appendix 3 of this book (page 131).

## STEPS TO MAKING SKILLS-FIRST HIRING A REALITY

To embrace skills-first hiring, organizations must undergo some important changes in their recruitment processes and cultural mindset. This involves:

1.  *Redefining Job Requirements*: Identify the core skills and competencies essential for success in each role, focusing on what candidates must be able to do rather than their background or traditional credentials. This process should start with a job analysis (covered later in the book). For large companies, this might involve a wholesale review of all job descriptions to ensure that unnecessary educational requirements are no longer listed as "required."

2.  *Implementing Skills Assessments*: Incorporate validated skill and competency assessments, simulations, and practical exercises into the hiring process to evaluate candidates' abilities accurately. An important factor for this step is to ensure that the assessments are valid and relevant for the jobs. Replacing unnecessary educational requirements with unnecessary assessed skills would be a poor choice.

3. *Identifying Alternative Credentials*: Consider available certifications and other credentials that verify that the candidates have the skills needed for the job. Some certifications are rigorously created and difficult to attain, while others are easy to attain and lack rigor. Good alternative credentials should be accredited by outside agencies and include an assessment to ensure that each individual has the proper skills. If there are credentials that show a level of knowledge or skills similar to an education degree, they should be used as alternative qualifications for job applicants. For example, the PMP certification from the Project Manager Institute is a well-known credential that can show companies that an applicant has skills as a project manager. While less conventional, this approach to alternative credentials aligns with a skills-first mindset and can offer several benefits to organizations.[7]

4. *Training Hiring Managers*: Equip hiring managers, like yourself, with the tools and training necessary to assess skills effectively and make unbiased hiring decisions. This will often involve using structured interviews and decision-making training. This training should also continue to emphasize the benefits of skills-first hiring for organizations.

5. *Promoting Diversity and Inclusion*: Foster a culture of diversity and inclusion by actively seeking out candidates from diverse backgrounds and creating equitable opportunities for all. Companies might need to fully reconsider where they are advertising their open roles and recruiting talent to ensure strong diversity in their talent acquisition pipeline.

6. *Emphasizing Continuous Improvement*: Regularly review and refine the skills-first hiring process based on feedback and outcomes, adapting to changing business needs and industry trends. As an organization changes to a skills-first hiring approach, they must continue to learn what is and is not working. And in terms of testing technical skills, the hiring process needs to stay on pace with the reality of jobs. Assessments should match what is done on the job. As technology changes, the assessment process should also be updated.

## COMMON MISCONCEPTIONS AND CHALLENGES TO A SKILLS-FIRST HIRING APPROACH

A skills-first hiring approach has several advantages, but it also comes with its own set of challenges and misconceptions. One common misconception is that <u>solely</u> focusing on skills overlooks other crucial factors such as a candidate's cultural fit, personality traits, and growth potential. Technical skills certainly matter for many jobs, but they should be considered alongside other factors to ensure that candidates are a good fit for the role and the entire organization. When I use the term "skills" in skills-first hiring, it is not meant to exclude other relevant competencies.

Another challenge of a skills-first hiring approach is the possibility of overlooking candidates who may not have specific technical skills but possess valuable transferable skills, aptitude, or potential for learning and development. I agree that relying too heavily on technical requirements can limit the talent pool and exclude individuals who could bring unique perspectives and experiences to the team. We should assess and consider all relevant factors that go into whether someone is most qualified for a job, including such factors as learning orientation.

Assessing candidate skills accurately during the hiring process can be difficult, especially in industries where skill requirements are regularly evolving or difficult to quantify. Employers may find it challenging to evaluate candidate proficiency in certain technical areas or predict their performance in the role based on traditional screening methods. However, there are good assessments of learning ability and willingness to learn that could be useful additions to the assessment process. Companies should explore whether these would be valid additions to the hiring process.

Further, some organizations may assume that a skills-first hiring approach is time-consuming and resource-intensive. Managers in these companies may see the process of assessing candidates' skills through assessments or tests as burdensome or impractical, particularly when faced with high volumes of applicants or tight hiring timelines. However, many assessments are available online and easy to administer quickly, so this concern could be based on previous experiences with outdated assessments.

Lastly, other managers or stakeholders may be resistant or skeptical about the transition to a skills-first approach. They may be more accustomed to traditional hiring methods focused on education, experience, or credentials. Educating these individuals about the value and effectiveness of a skills-first approach and addressing any concerns or misconceptions can help garner support for the transition.

## CHAPTER SUMMARY

Skills-first hiring is a new way of recruiting that can help organizations improve by way of their talent acquisition processes. This approach prioritizes skills over other factors, such as education or experience, to find the best candidates for the job. By doing this, organizations can unlock the full potential of their workforce, promote diversity, improve performance, and enhance resilience. This shift can help organizations succeed in a competitive and ever-changing business environment, as long as they are willing to make necessary changes.

FOR MORE INFORMATION

1. Study from Harvard Business School: https://www.hbs.edu/managing-the-future-of-work/Documents/dismissed-by-degrees.pdf
2. Sigelman, M., Fuller, J., Martin, A. (February 2024). Skills-Based Hiring: The Long Road from Pronouncements to Practice. Published by Burning Glass Institute.
3. More information about IBM's New Collar initiative can be found here: https://www.ibm.com/impact/feature/apprenticeship
4. More information about Airbnb's skills-based hiring can be found here: https://www.tryexponent.com/blog/airbnb-interview-process
5. More information about Google's skills-first hiring can be found here: https://www.google.com/about/careers/applications/how-we-hire/
6. More information about Amazon's Career Choice program can be found here: https://www.amazoncareerchoice.com/
7. For more information about using skilled credentials for hiring, see these resources from the SHRM Foundation: https://www.shrm.org/foundation/skilled-credentials

25

*Acquiring the right talent
is the most important key
to growth. Hiring was –
and still is – the most
important thing we do.*

Mark Benioff (Salesforce)

# CHAPTER 3

# THE TALENT ACQUISITION FUNNEL

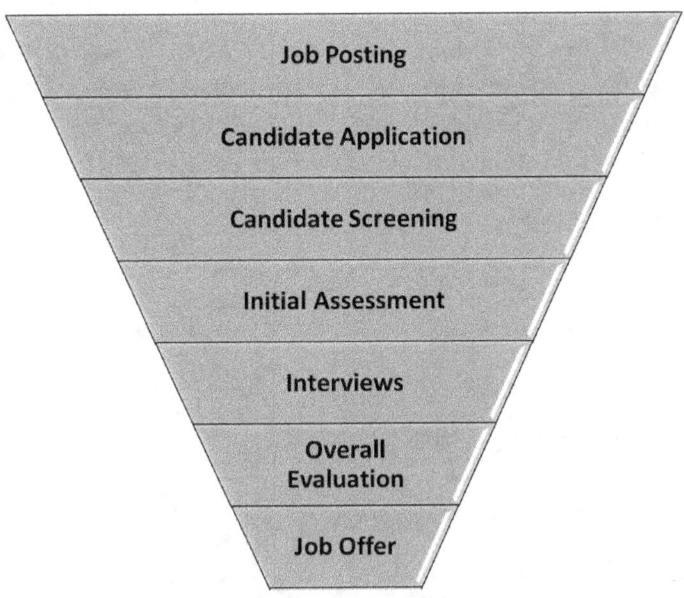


## What the Hiring Manager Needs to Remember

Many companies follow a common multi-step process to select the most qualified candidate for their roles. The process begins by posting the job in places where the most potentially qualified applicants are. This step also considers how to find diverse candidates who may not have been aware of the opportunity previously. After that, the applicants are screened and assessed in various ways to determine which ones are most likely to succeed. This often includes computer-based tests, as well as interviews. By using a standard process for evaluating candidates, organizations can ensure compliance with laws and best practices and help to promote fairness.

L et's explore the world of talent acquisition! Imagine your company's hiring process as a funnel, starting with a wide pool of potential applicants and gradually narrowing down to find the perfect fit for the role. At each stage of this funnel, candidates go through different steps that help us evaluate their suitability for the job. Some steps require action from the candidates themselves, while others involve decisions made by the hiring organization.

In this chapter, we'll take a closer look at each part of the candidate funnel, giving you a sneak peek into what to expect. And don't worry—we'll dive deeper into the key steps in later chapters, so you'll have all the insights you need to help streamline your hiring process and emphasize a skills-first approach.

Here's an example of such a funnel:

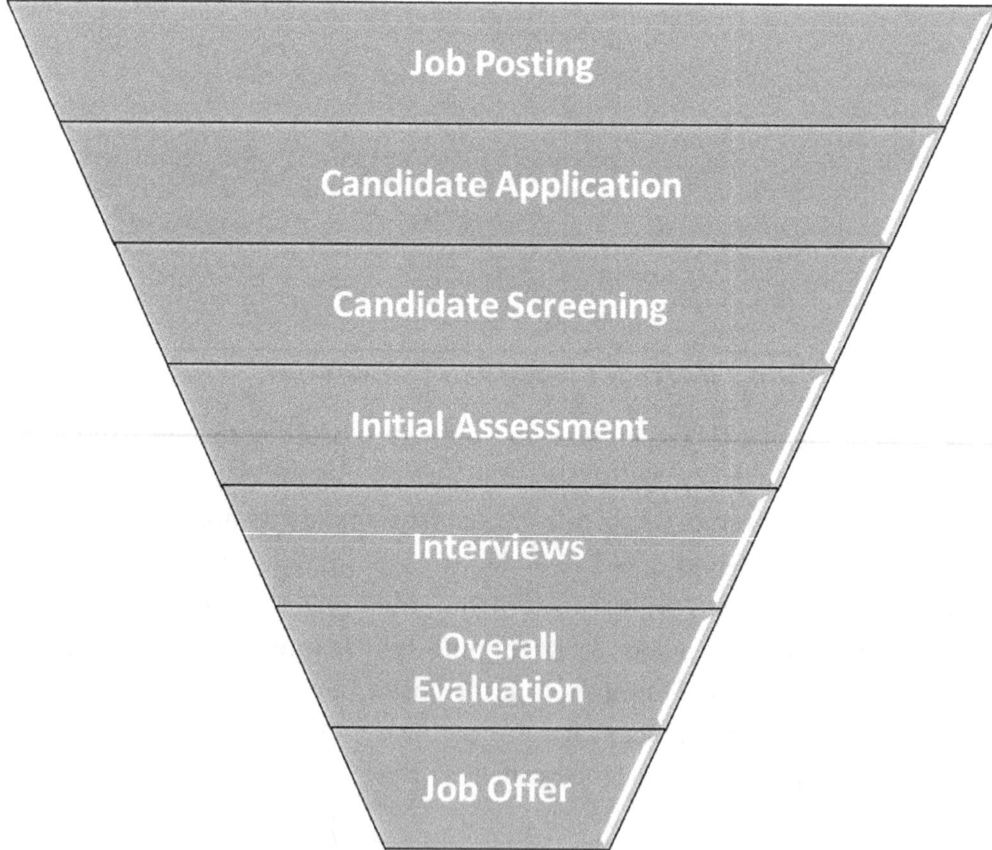

As candidates move through each stage of the funnel during the recruiting and hiring process, the pool of candidates narrows down until the right final hire is identified, hired, and starts as a new employee. This process helps ensure that the organization considers a wide range of candidates but hires the most qualified and best candidate for the job. It also helps to standardize the process and ensure that all candidates are treated fairly as they are considered for the role.

# 1. JOB POSTING

The top stage in the funnel involves informing and attracting potential candidates to the job opening through various channels such as job boards, social media, company careers page, employee referrals, and networking events.

There are large general job boards (such as www.indeed.com or www.monster.com) that most companies use. These are relatively cheap and typical places that the broadest range of organizations use for their job postings. Placing job postings in these locations helps to ensure that the widest group of potential applicants is aware of the position.

In addition, many specialty sites are good for finding candidates from niche areas. For instance, professional associations will often have areas on their websites for job postings that are only relevant to members of that profession. You might be more aware of these specialty sites than your talent acquisition partner, so you should be sure to suggest the most appropriate ones for your job postings.

You should also look to place job postings in locations that diverse candidates will see. This includes reaching out to specialized job boards, attending diversity-focused career fairs, and leveraging social media channels with diverse audiences. Additionally, fostering partnerships with diversity and inclusion organizations can enhance visibility among underrepresented groups.

## EMPLOYEE REFERRALS

Employee referrals are an important way of attracting candidates that are worthy of your consideration. Good research studies have demonstrated the benefits of referral programs[1]. Specifically, these studies show that candidates who are referred by current employees tend to stay longer in the organization and end up being better job performers. There are a couple of potential reasons for this. One is that your current employees will likely refer people whom they think will perform and fit well with the organization. As a result, using a referral process works as an easy pre-screening step. Another potential reason is that the new hire will have at least one existing relationship with someone in the organization, so they might be able to navigate the new organization better than others without a friend at work. This prior relationship might give them access to information that others do not have (which can help their job performance). The relationship might also make them want to stay in the organization longer than others.

Despite the documented benefits of employee referrals, there are some serious concerns about them. This typically occurs for diversity and equity reasons. The idea is that employee referrals will likely share the same backgrounds (including demographics) as current employees. As a result, new employees who are referred by current employees might end up making the company more similar (less diverse) over time. Further, employees with prior relationships might have advantages that are unfair and also work against diversity and inclusion goals.

As a hiring manager, you should stay on top of this referral/diversity issue. The benefits of referrals are known, but if referrals are leading to less diversity than the broader job market, you need to do something about it. Such things might include simple communications to the team about diversity considerations in the referral process or adding incentives for referrals who add diversity to the team. It would be a shame to let go of the merits of employee referrals because of this potentially fixable issue.


## 2. CANDIDATE APPLICATION

Candidates who are interested in the job opportunity submit their applications using designated methods, such as an online application portal or email. Many companies have been able to automate most of this process in recent years using different systems, saving a lot of recruiter time and effort.

At this point, I should note two of the biggest complaints for job seekers in the recruitment process. The first involves the replication of information that is asked of candidates. Companies often ask for traditional resumes and then require candidates to enter that same information separately into their applicant tracking system (ATS). This can be a big waste of time and effort for candidates and often leads otherwise qualified individuals to drop out of the application process altogether. As a hiring manager, you should address this with the talent acquisition person/team. Even if you are in a small company, asking candidates for redundant information is a big turn-off. The good news is that AI programs are now available and can read and interpret unstructured data, such as information presented in resumes. By using this technology (which is quickly being incorporated into many applicant tracking systems), you can avoid the redundant requests that are huge turn-offs for job seekers.

Another common complaint from job seekers is the fact that many times they enter their resume and other information and never hear back from the company. This seems to occur even when candidates meet all the posted requirements for the job. This lack of communication early in the recruiting process can taint applicant views of the organization. This is particularly relevant for consumer-facing brands and companies (e.g., clothing stores) that have largely overlapping customer and applicant groups. In these situations, keeping their applicants happy will also help keep their customers happy.

Therefore, it is incumbent on you to ensure that there is a communication and response plan for all your job applicants. If you have a recruiter, you typically do not have to be involved at this point. However, you should check to make sure that good and consistent candidate communications are in place.

## 3. CANDIDATE SCREENING

In this stage of the process, you or a recruiter review the applications or resumes to screen out unqualified candidates based on basic criteria such as experience, credentials, and skills. For many jobs, education has been a common screening criterion, although I maintain that this can be a mistake based on the skills-first hiring approach if the education degree does not demonstrate that a person has job-relevant skills.

As with coordinating the candidate application, large parts of this step can now be outsourced to technology. Specifically (as I mentioned above), systems using AI can read and understand information from various sources and in different formats better than it ever has. This technology can save a lot of time and attention by automatically weeding out the candidates who lack the skills and competencies for the role.

Note that hiring managers in most larger companies have very little input on what goes on in this step. However, HR/talent acquisition (if you have them) should be willing to share with you their candidate screening methods and goals for this step in the hiring process.

## 4. INITIAL ASSESSMENT

Next, applicants who pass the previous step often undergo some type of initial assessment. This may include online tests, automated phone screenings, or preliminary interviews (often automated in nature) to evaluate their fit for the role. In many cases, these tests are referred to as "psychometric assessments." As these assessments have become computerized and easy to administer, they have become popular tools used by companies to screen candidates. These assessments are designed to measure various psychological traits, abilities, and skills that should be relevant to the job.

If your company is not using computerized assessments, I strongly recommend considering them to help identify good candidates. If they are created well and properly validated, they can play an important role in determining which candidates are qualified by directly assessing their skills.

One type of assessment commonly used by companies is a cognitive ability test. These tests evaluate candidates' mental aptitude in areas such as verbal reasoning, numerical reasoning, and logical thinking. By assessing candidates' problem-solving skills and critical thinking abilities, these tests help predict the potential to succeed in the job role. As we will discuss in later chapters, these assessments have consistently shown that they can be valid predictors of who will perform the job well. However, they have legal concerns and diversity challenges which need to be addressed.

Personality assessments are another type of psychometric assessment used in the hiring process for many companies. These assessments are designed to measure candidate behavioral traits, values, and preferences to evaluate their fit with the job role and organizational culture. Note that even though candidate faking on these assessments is a concern, they can still be valuable screening tools – particularly if more sophisticated items are used.

Additionally, some companies use situational judgment tests (SJTs) to assess candidate decision-making and judgment in work-related scenarios. SJTs present candidates with realistic workplace situations and ask them to choose the most appropriate course of action. These assessments can help you evaluate candidates' problem-solving abilities, ethical judgment, and decision-making skills in relevant and practical contexts.

Today, many of these assessments can be outsourced to technology. From scheduling tests to conducting and scoring the assessments, little human time and attention are required if the right technology is used. Also, I should note that companies typically use short assessments at this phase of the hiring process. Older assessments tended to be rather long (20-30 minutes for a test was common). However, most newer assessments are much shorter (less than 10 minutes) and more focused in content.

## BRIEF SUMMARY OF U.S. LAWS AND REGULATIONS FOR EMPLOYMENT SCREENING

In the United States, there is a set of laws and regulations that companies should be aware of when considering employment screening methods and other assessments.

The **Uniform Guidelines on Employee Selection Procedures** were published in 1978 by a collection of U.S. government agencies. They provide a set of common standards to help define and promote fairness and to prevent discrimination in employee testing. They cover various testing procedures, including interviews, tests, and other assessments. Importantly, the guidelines introduce the idea of *disparate* **treatment** between demographic groups and mandate that all groups should be treated fairly and equally. Companies should have rules and standards for tests and assessments that are documented and followed consistently.

In addition, these guidelines discuss the *disparate **impact*** of testing, which is the idea that different groups might be differentially hired using the tests, even when all applicants are treated equally. Disparate impact is not necessarily against these guidelines, but companies are obligated to demonstrate that the tests are valid if they show disparate impact. In this case, a demonstration of validity would involve evidence that the tests are necessary and job-relevant.

In addition, several other U.S. laws and regulations govern employee testing. Some key ones include:

1. **Civil Rights Act of 1964** (Title VII): Prohibits employment discrimination based on race, color, religion, sex, or national origin.

2. **Americans with Disabilities Act** (ADA): Ensures equal opportunities for individuals with disabilities and restricts the use of certain medical examinations or inquiries.

3. **Age Discrimination in Employment Act** (ADEA): Prohibits age discrimination against individuals who are 40 years or older.

Compliance with these laws is crucial to creating fair and unbiased employee screening and assessment procedures. More information about these laws, as well as legal issues with hiring in countries outside of the U.S., is available in the Appendix (page 123 for U.S. laws and page 127 for non-U.S. laws).

## 5. INTERVIEWS

A relatively small number of final candidates proceed to the interview stage, where they may undergo multiple rounds of interviews with different stakeholders. This usually includes you, other team members, and senior management. Note that I consider computerized and depersonalized "interviews" (where candidates are speaking to a computer program or simply recording themselves) a type of psychometric assessment (covered above), rather than an interview. This is not to diminish their effectiveness in the applicant screening process, but it is important to establish reasonable definitions.

Interviews by their nature are two-way interactions. Even though we might think of them as just another part of the candidate evaluation process, candidates often value them as a way of getting to know the manager and other members of the work team. As a result, interviewers need to be friendly, helpful, and engaging. After all, you still need the candidate that you select to actually accept the role and want to work with you.

## THE BENEFITS OF STRUCTURED V. UNSTRUCTURED INTERVIEWS

At this point, it is important to bring up key research findings about the validity of job interviews. A series of research studies have conclusively shown that *structured* interviews are quite valid and good predictors of which candidates will ultimately be successful on the job[2]. Structured interviews take quite a bit of time and effort to create consistency – both in the questions asked in the interviews and the ways that the interview responses are evaluated.

On the other hand, unstructured interviews are **not** good ways of evaluating candidates for jobs[3]. Unstructured interviews are quite common and typically involve little or no preparation on the part of the interviewers.

---

Interviews should be consistent and structured to ensure fair and valid evaluations of candidates.

---

As a hiring manager, you should be ready for HR/talent acquisition to provide you with a standard set of interview questions and ways to evaluate candidates. Please know that this is done for the benefit of everyone (even though this level of structure might not suit you on a personal level). If you do not have HR or talent acquisition professionals, you should take the time to plan the interview questions and the ways that you will evaluate candidate responses. Even though this involves additional preparation for you, it will help you accurately assess the final candidates.

## 6. OVERALL EVALUATION AND DECISION

After the interviews, final candidates are evaluated based on their overall profile, skills, experience, cultural fit, and other relevant factors to determine their suitability for the role and the organization. Even though input often comes from multiple sources, you will likely have the final say about the hiring decision.

That is why I want you – as the hiring manager – to pay close attention to this section and the related sections in this book.

There is a common problem at this stage for most hiring managers. Many of you are poorly equipped to make the final determination of who is the best fit for the role. You might get a good "feel" for people in some situations, but this is an important decision that requires evidence-based insight and a close focus on relevant information.

As a result of this issue with the final candidate evaluation, delays in the hiring process often occur. This can result in missed opportunities to hire top candidates with other offers, as well as lost time and momentum (and often revenue) as the job remains unfilled. A recent economic research study helped address this issue and answer the question of how much hiring delays hurt financial performance[4]. Their results showed that doubling the time it takes to fill a vacant role leads to a three percent drop in profits. Further, a company facing even an average amount of hiring difficulty can expect a five percent drop in sales compared to a company with no delays.

<hr>

Hiring delays cost companies lots of money.

<hr>

As I analyze the situation, there are a couple of common reasons why hiring managers often have a tough time making the final hiring decision:

1.  There is a lack of clarity about the role and relevant success factors in the organization.
2.  Final candidates are very similar to each other.
3.  There is missing information about the relevant competencies of the final candidates.

As a hiring manager, you must ensure that you have clarity about your organization, the role, and the final candidates. If you do not have the right information or are not comfortable with deciding this point in the process, you need to determine what information you lack.

*How would you get this additional information to make a good final hiring decision?* We will cover this in a later chapter.

## 7. JOB OFFER

The top candidate receives a job offer, which includes details such as compensation, benefits, start date, and other relevant terms. Negotiations may occur at this stage.

## NEXT STEPS: ACCEPTANCE AND ONBOARDING

Once an offer is extended, the candidate decides whether to accept or decline the offer. If accepted, the candidate formally joins the organization and begins the onboarding process. The final stage involves integrating the new hire into the organization through orientation, training, and other onboarding activities to ensure a smooth transition and set them up for success in their new role.

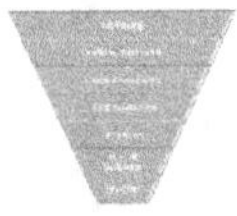

## CHAPTER SUMMARY

The talent acquisition funnel is a model that shows the process that most organizations use to determine the best job candidates. This involves multiple discrete steps including 1) job posting, 2) candidate application, 3) candidate screening, 4) initial assessment, 5) interviews, 6) overall evaluation, 7) job offer, and 8) acceptance and onboarding. Care should be taken at each step to communicate effectively with candidates and ensure that all candidates are evaluated fairly. If these things are not addressed, good candidates might drop out of the process – and you could run afoul of laws and regulations.

Mark A. Smith, Ph.D.


FOR MORE INFORMATION

1. Le Barbanchon, Thomas, Maddalena Ronchi, and Julien Sauvagnat. 2023. "Hiring Difficulties and Firm Growth." CEPR Discussion Paper No. 17891. CEPR Press, Paris & London.
2. Sackett, P. R., Zhang, C., Berry, C. M., & Lievens, F. (2022). Revisiting meta-analytic estimates of validity in personnel selection: Addressing systematic overcorrection for restriction of range. *Journal of Applied Psychology*, 107(11), 2040–2068. https://doi.org/10.1037/apl0000994
3. Campion, M. A., Palmer, D. K., & Campion, J. E. (1997). A Review of Structure in the Selection Interview. *Personnel Psychology,* 50, 655–702. https://doi.org/doi.org/10.1111/j.1744-6570.1997.tb00709.
4. Stephen V. Burks, Bo Cowgill, Mitchell Hoffman, Michael Housman (2015). *The Quarterly Journal of Economics*, Volume 130, Issue 2, May, Pages 805–839, https://doi.org/10.1093/qje/qjv010

39

*How can you run for
president if you don't know
the job description?*

Mohamed ElBaradei

# CHAPTER 4

# DEFINING CORE JOB SKILLS AND WRITING JOB DESCRIPTIONS

- Identifying Essential Skills for Your Jobs and Organization

- Technical vs. Soft Skills: Finding the Right Balance

- Assessing Skills Gaps and Future Needs

**What the Hiring Manager Needs to Remember**

After a job opening is approved, you need to determine what the role involves and what success in the role looks like. In many cases, older job descriptions will already exist for the position. However, existing job descriptions are often outdated and even misleading. As the hiring manager, you must ensure that you have a current and proper understanding of the role (both the duties and tasks, as well as the required competencies). And then you need to make sure that these are appropriately documented in the job description. Some thought and preparation at this early stage will help you greatly later in the hiring process.

Welcome to the important stage of defining your job roles and crafting job descriptions! Before you jump into the hiring process and start evaluating candidates, it's essential to take a step back and carefully evaluate the role you're looking to fill. All too often, hiring processes stumble right out of the gate because the role wasn't fully understood or the job posting lacked crucial details.

In this chapter, we'll walk you through the process of evaluating your roles to pinpoint the key skills and competencies needed. Plus, we'll dive into the art of crafting job descriptions that are not only accurate but also enticing to potential candidates.

## IDENTIFYING REQUIRED SKILLS AND COMPETENCIES

Identifying core skills to include in job descriptions is crucial for attracting qualified candidates who possess the capabilities to excel in the role. This process involves a comprehensive analysis of the job requirements, considering both technical proficiencies and soft skills, while also anticipating future needs of the job.

Here is how to effectively identify and prioritize core skills and competencies for job descriptions:

### 1. CONDUCT A JOB TASK ANALYSIS

Begin by conducting a thorough job analysis to understand the responsibilities, tasks, and objectives of the role. This is typically done by talking with job experts, reviewing materials, and collecting task survey information. A full job analysis does not have to be done every time – particularly for roles that are regularly hired. However, a job analysis should be updated every two or three years, with even greater frequency for roles that are fluid and change regularly.

If a job is new or has no existing job analysis information, the O*Net (onetonline.org) from the U.S. Department of Labor/Employment and Training Administration is a great place to find relevant information for thousands of jobs.

If you go to the website and search for jobs, you will almost certainly find good information that is relevant to your open role. However, note that you should use O*Net information as a starting point and take steps to ensure that you only accept task and competency information that is relevant to your role and organization. This may involve asking other job experts to review it for accuracy and relevance for your company.

*Example O*Net information:* https://www.onetonline.org/link/summary/29-1292.00

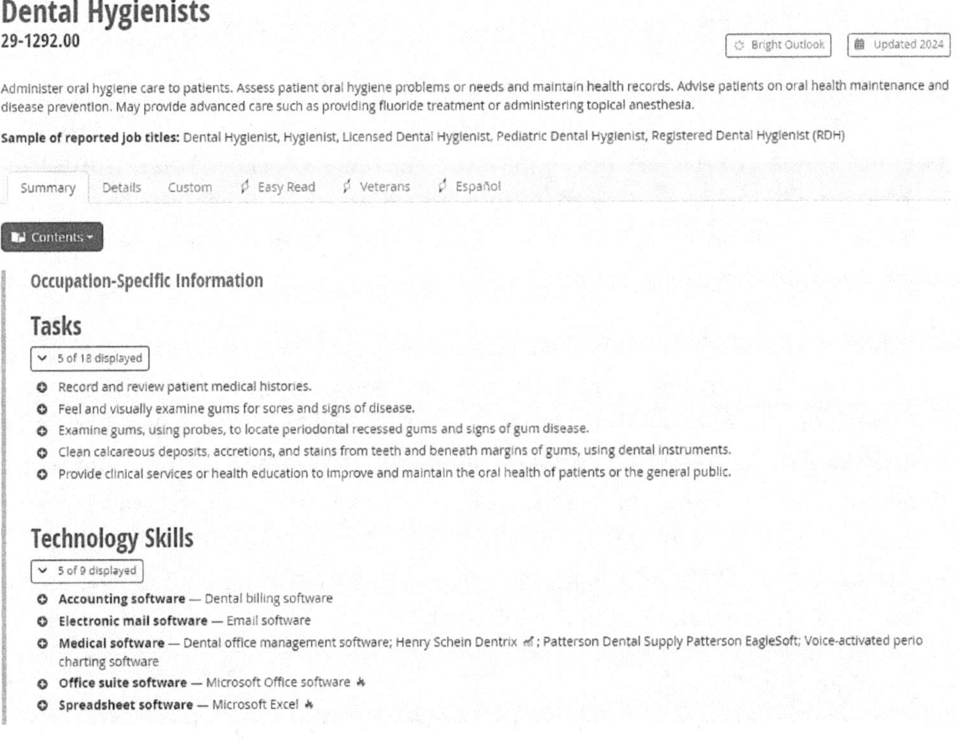

## Dental Hygienists

**29-1292.00**

| ☼ Bright Outlook | 🏛 Updated 2024 |

Administer oral hygiene care to patients. Assess patient oral hygiene problems or needs and maintain health records. Advise patients on oral health maintenance and disease prevention. May provide advanced care such as providing fluoride treatment or administering topical anesthesia.

**Sample of reported job titles:** Dental Hygienist, Hygienist, Licensed Dental Hygienist, Pediatric Dental Hygienist, Registered Dental Hygienist (RDH)

Summary  Details  Custom  ∅ Easy Read  ∅ Veterans  ∅ Español

📑 Contents ▾

### Occupation-Specific Information

## Tasks

⌄ 5 of 18 displayed

- ⊕ Record and review patient medical histories.
- ⊕ Feel and visually examine gums for sores and signs of disease.
- ⊕ Examine gums, using probes, to locate periodontal recessed gums and signs of gum disease.
- ⊕ Clean calcareous deposits, accretions, and stains from teeth and beneath margins of gums, using dental instruments.
- ⊕ Provide clinical services or health education to improve and maintain the oral health of patients or the general public.

## Technology Skills

⌄ 5 of 9 displayed

- ⊕ **Accounting software** — Dental billing software
- ⊕ **Electronic mail software** — Email software
- ⊕ **Medical software** — Dental office management software; Henry Schein Dentrix ◪ ; Patterson Dental Supply Patterson EagleSoft; Voice-activated perio charting software
- ⊕ **Office suite software** — Microsoft Office software ♣
- ⊕ **Spreadsheet software** — Microsoft Excel ♣

A good job analysis should also involve reviewing existing job descriptions, consulting with subject matter experts, and observing current employees in similar positions. As much as possible, this process should be standard, rigorous, and collected from multiple sources.

In addition, collecting task and competency ratings on job analysis surveys is often part of this process. We often use ratings from these surveys to help document the results in numerical format so that we can rank-order the responsibilities, tasks, and objectives of the role by frequency or importance. The results from the job analysis provide a great start for identifying core skills that will provide the basis for an accurate job description.

## 2. Identify Technical Skills

Technical skills refer to the specific competencies and proficiencies required to perform job-related tasks effectively. These may include such things as software proficiency, industry-specific skills, programming languages, machinery operation, or other specialized knowledge. Information from O*Net and the job analysis can also help you fully consider the technical requirements of the role and prioritize those skills that are essential for success.

Further, technical skills should be "linked" to tasks that are documented as part of the job via the job analysis. That is, you should be able to cite specific tasks that are part of the job that require specific technical skills. This ensures that you only include technical skills that are used in important aspects of the job. If a skill cannot be linked to important job tasks/duties, then it should probably be omitted from the list of relevant skills.

## 3. Consider Important Soft Skills

In addition to technical skills, soft skills and competencies often play a vital role in determining an individual's success in a job. Soft skills, also known as interpersonal or people skills, include traits such as communication, teamwork, adaptability, and leadership. In this process, you should consider how the role interacts with other roles and identify the soft skills that are critical for effective performance and collaboration. As with technical skills, soft skills should be linked to tasks that are documented in the job analysis.

## 4. Anticipate Future Needs

As jobs continue to evolve and industries undergo transformation, it is also a good idea to look ahead. Try to anticipate future needs and incorporate relevant skills into job descriptions. Consider emerging trends, technological advancements, and changes in market demands that may impact the role. This proactive approach will help ensure that job descriptions remain relevant when taking evolving business needs into account. However, remember that these anticipated needs are simply educated guesses and should be evaluated and reconsidered regularly.

## 5. PRIORITIZE CORE SKILLS

Once you have identified a comprehensive list of technical and soft skills that are job-relevant, prioritize them based on their relevance to the role and their impact on job performance. If you have job analysis survey data, prioritizing the results is easy. For the job description, be sure to focus on the core skills that are most essential for success. Also, you can include secondary skills that may enhance a candidate's suitability or potential for growth within the organization, but you should list them separately from the core skills in the job description.

## 6. TAILOR TO THE ORGANIZATION'S CULTURE AND VALUES

In addition to factors relevant to the specific roles, you should also consider the organization's culture, values, and mission when identifying and documenting key skills and competencies for job descriptions. Seek alignment between the required skills and the nature of the organization to ensure that candidates who possess both technical competencies and cultural fit are attracted to the role.

## 7. GATHER ADDITIONAL INPUT FROM STAKEHOLDERS

After creating draft lists of core skills and other information for the job description, it is a good idea to share with relevant stakeholders, including other managers, team members, and senior leadership. This will allow you to validate and refine the list of required skills for the job description. Their insights and perspectives can provide valuable input into the identification and prioritization of skills based on their firsthand knowledge of the role and its requirements.

*Summary*: Identifying required skills and competencies to include in job descriptions requires a thoughtful and systematic approach that considers both technical proficiencies and soft skills, while also anticipating the future needs of the job. By conducting a thorough job task analysis, considering the organization's culture, and seeking input from stakeholders, organizations can create job descriptions that attract the right candidates and set the stage for success in the recruitment process.

# CRAFTING EFFECTIVE JOB DESCRIPTIONS

As the primary decision-maker responsible for filling the position, you play a crucial role in crafting effective job descriptions for job postings. This involves stating the requirements, responsibilities, and qualifications necessary for success in the role. In most medium-sized and larger companies, a recruiter or talent acquisition professional can help with this step. However, managers in smaller companies are often on their own in developing job descriptions.

Here's a closer look at the steps in this process, with a focus on your role as the hiring manager:

## 1. DOCUMENTING THE JOB REQUIREMENTS

You should start with a comprehensive understanding of the job requirements, including the specific skills and competencies needed to excel in the role. As documented in the previous section, this involves conducting a thorough analysis of the job function, its place within the organization, and the desired outcomes. For jobs that are frequently filled, this is usually a straightforward process. For specialized or unique jobs, this can be tricky and less certain.

## 2. LISTING THE KEY RESPONSIBILITIES

Based on your understanding of the job requirements, you should identify and prioritize the key responsibilities and tasks associated with the role. This involves distinguishing between essential duties and secondary ones. It should not be a complete list of all job responsibilities. Including too many job duties is a common mistake that I see in job descriptions. I recommend including no more than ten responsibilities in a job posting. Focusing on the most important ones will ensure that the job description accurately reflects the core functions of the position.

## 3. STATING QUALIFICATIONS AND REQUIREMENTS

You are responsible for clearly listing the qualifications and skills necessary for the role. This may include specifying educational requirements, technical proficiencies, certifications, and any other relevant criteria that candidates must meet to be considered for the position.

Note that for a skills-first hiring approach, specific educational requirements should be carefully evaluated before being used in the job descriptions. In some cases, college or traditional education is the only place where most people can develop the skills and knowledge necessary for the job. If so, requiring a specific college degree (often an advanced degree) makes sense. But for many jobs, college is just one of several places where job-relevant skills can be developed. For instance, sales roles often include college degree requirements, but most college majors (even relevant ones like Communications) focus on skills that are not directly related to a sales job.

We live in the Information Age. There are many widely available videos, podcasts, reports, blog posts, etc. that can provide solid training on all sorts of knowledge and skills. If you decide to include college degree requirements in job postings, I encourage you to include alternative paths that would lead to similar levels of knowledge/skill. For instance, there might be a certification that shows that a candidate has a level of knowledge equivalent to a college degree. For example, HR certifications from HRCI and SHRM cover knowledge of key aspects of human resources and demonstrate an individual's knowledge in these areas. Although using college degrees and alternative credentials might not be common, this practice can benefit organizations by expanding the candidate pool.

## 4. WRITING CLEAR AND ENGAGING DESCRIPTIONS

Crafting compelling job descriptions that resonate with potential candidates is an important step for attracting top talent. Job descriptions should include clear, concise language and avoid jargon or industry-specific terms that may be unfamiliar to some candidates. Additionally, they should highlight the unique aspects of the role and the organization to differentiate it from similar opportunities in the market. Hopefully, a talent acquisition professional is available to help with this, as writing clear and engaging job descriptions is not the strong suit of every hiring manager.

You should also be sure to include information about your Employer Value Proposition (EVP) that will help to make you attractive to good candidates. If you work in a larger company, a talent acquisition professional should be able to explain the EVP for your organization and help with this process.

## 5. ENSURING INCLUSIVE LANGUAGE

Job descriptions should also be inclusive and accessible to candidates from diverse backgrounds. This involves using inclusive language, avoiding biased or discriminatory terms, and considering alternative qualifications or experiences that may contribute to success in the role.

Below is a table that has some example terms that should generally be avoided and ways of discussing these things with more inclusive terminology.

| Terms to Avoid | Alternative, Inclusive Terms |
| --- | --- |
| Man/Men | People, individuals, candidates |
| Chairman/Chairmen | Chair, chairperson, chairing |
| Salesman/Salesmen | Sales representative, salesperson |
| Policeman | Law enforcement officer, police officer |
| Fireman | Firefighter, fire personnel |
| Waitress | Server, waitstaff |
| Maiden name | Birth name |
| Disabled/Handicapped | Person with disabilities |
| Illegal Alien | Undocumented immigrant, migrant worker |
| Foreigner | International applicant, non-native |

## 6. COLLABORATING WITH STAKEHOLDERS

Creating good job descriptions often requires collaboration with various stakeholders, including other team members and senior leadership. You should use this time to seek input and feedback from relevant parties to ensure that the job description accurately reflects the needs and expectations of the organization.

## 7. REGULAR REVIEW AND UPDATES

Job descriptions should be reviewed regularly to ensure that they remain accurate and updated with current business needs and industry trends. Typically, I recommend that job descriptions be updated annually or whenever they are used for a new job posting. This is particularly important when relevant skills are in a constant state of change. You should take the initiative in reviewing and revising job descriptions as necessary.

For many companies who are adopting a skills-first hiring approach, a comprehensive review of existing job descriptions is one of the first steps. This allows them to understand how many of their job descriptions list required college degrees so they can discuss which are truly *necessary* requirements and which should be eliminated. And if they are eliminated, you can have a more comprehensive discussion about alternative ways of describing the job requirements to make it more inclusive of ways in which relevant skills can be acquired. This would include a discussion of alternative credentials that could be used in the screening process as equivalent to a college degree.

## CHAPTER SUMMARY

In summary, the hiring manager plays a central role in identifying core job skills and crafting effective job descriptions for job postings. By understanding the job requirements, articulating clear responsibilities and qualifications, and ensuring inclusivity and collaboration, the organization can attract qualified candidates and set the stage for a successful recruitment process. Even though it takes a level of effort to collect and use this information, this is an important part of the overall talent acquisition process.

*Somebody once said that in looking for people to hire, you look for three qualities: integrity, intelligence, and energy. and if you don't have the first, the other two will kill you.*

Warren Buffet

# CHAPTER 5

# ASSESSMENT AND SCREENING PROCESS

- Using Tools and Techniques for Skill Assessment

- Ensuring the Use of Valid Assessments in the Screening Process

- Brief Review of US Legal and Regulatory Guidelines for Hiring Tests

<table>
<tr><td>What the Hiring Manager Needs to Remember</td></tr>
<tr><td>

Many methods of candidate assessment are available for organizations. Most of these assessments are now computerized and easy to use. However, many have <u>not</u> demonstrated that they are useful in the applicant screening process – particularly for each role that you are considering. As the hiring manager, you should ask the right questions about your assessments to make sure that they are valid for the role. And if they do not have evidence of validity, you might consider ways of collecting this evidence. Testing companies have many available assessments that can evaluate candidates in a standard way. But it is up to you to make sure that it is done in ways that will provide you with the most benefit and will keep you in line with laws and regulations.

</td></tr>
</table>

In the quest to find the perfect candidate, assessment tools are your trusty sidekicks, helping you evaluate qualifications, skills, and overall fit for the role. From the tried-and-true methods like resume reviews and interviews to cutting-edge assessments and technologies, there are a bunch of options for you. Valid assessments are particularly important in skills-first hiring when education level is not used to screen out candidates.

In this chapter, we'll take a closer look at these assessment procedures, exploring how they can help you find the ideal candidate for your open role. Plus, we'll dive into the importance of ensuring that these tools are reliable and valid in evaluating candidates for your open roles.

Here is an overview of some common applicant assessment and screening tools, along with real-world examples:

## 1. RESUME SCREENING

Resume reviews remain a fundamental tool for screening candidates, providing a snapshot of their education, work experience, skills, and accomplishments. Automated resume screening software can help hiring managers quickly filter through large volumes of resumes based on predefined criteria, such as keywords or certifications.

In the past decade, ATS (Applicant Tracking Systems) have become common in organizations and are useful in organizing candidate information for your open roles. And now, AI-based ATSs are used by many companies that can understand unformatted data taken directly from resumes. These programs can easily be used to determine who meets core job requirements. In addition, some programs can be used to score and rank candidate resumes based on more complex factors than they could use in the past. This is a good use of AI to help evaluate candidate work histories in a better way than just looking for keywords.

Importantly, ATS technology has become relatively affordable and usable so that even smaller companies benefit from using it. If you are not using an ATS and recruit for multiple jobs each year, I recommend that you look into adding an ATS to help you coordinate your hiring process.

Real-world examples:

ATS platforms like Greenhouse ([www.greenhouse.com](www.greenhouse.com)) and Lever ([www.lever.co](www.lever.co)) offer resume evaluation and screening capabilities, allowing you to efficiently manage and review candidate applications.

## 2. PRE-EMPLOYMENT ASSESSMENTS

Many companies use pre-employment assessments, such as personality tests, cognitive assessments, and skills assessments, to evaluate candidates' aptitude, behavior, and abilities relevant to the job. Most current assessments are computer-based, with some relying on more advanced technology than others. Good assessments provide valuable insights into candidates' suitability for the role and their potential for success.

Some assessments take just a few minutes to complete, while others are much longer. At the early stages of the hiring process, most companies use short assessments that are good at identifying general fit for specific roles. Also, candidates prefer to take assessments that can be done quickly. However, most short assessments are not able to describe applicants in any depth, as they look for very specific traits in applicants. On the other hand, longer assessments can measure many more psychological traits in a single test, which can be useful in understanding each individual. However, most of the measured traits will likely not be valid for screening candidates for your open roles. And, you run the risk of losing candidates early in the hiring process if you ask them to take a lengthy assessment.

For ease of use, most assessments are designed to directly interface with ATS platforms which allows for fast and seamless exchange of information. This type of ATS interaction is important and helps to create a quick evaluation process.

Real-world examples:

Companies like Xobin ([www.xobin.com](www.xobin.com)) and SHL ([www.shl.com](www.shl.com)) offer a wide range of pre-employment assessments, including cognitive ability tests, personality assessments, and job simulations, to help organizations make more informed hiring decisions.

*Example Candidate Assessment Results — Xobin*

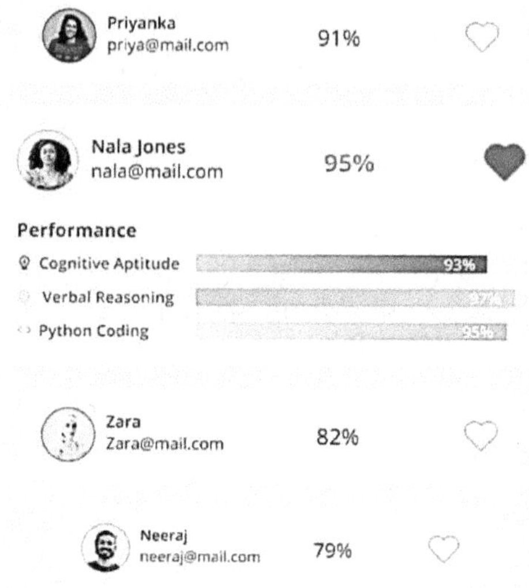


# 3. AUTOMATED VIDEO INTERVIEWS

Automated video interviews involve asking candidates standard questions and having candidates respond on video to their computer or other device. New versions of these interviews use AI-based technology to understand and score their responses. In many cases, situational or behavioral questions are used to assess candidates' past experiences, problem-solving abilities, and people skills. Recent research studies have shown that these automated interviews can be valid and useful additions to applicant screening processes.[1]

Similar to actual interviews, this approach often uses scenario or behavior-based questions to help organizations investigate how candidates might perform in real-world scenarios and how they have handled situations in the past. However, these automated interviews can be done at much greater volume and are quicker to schedule and conduct than standard interviews with people. But it is important to note that they do not involve the two-way interaction that traditional interviews offer — and because of this, I consider these automated interviews a specific type of assessment, rather than a type of interview.

## REAL-WORLD EXAMPLES:

Video interview platforms like HireVue (www.hirevue.com) and Spark Hire (www.sparkhire.com) enable organizations to conduct structured video interviews, automate the scheduling process, and review candidate responses asynchronously.

# 4. TECHNICAL SKILLS ASSESSMENTS

Skills-based assessments evaluate the technical skills and competencies of candidates and cover such things as coding tests for software engineers or case studies for business analysts. In many cases, skill assessments can match job tasks and allow candidates to demonstrate their relevant skills in a very direct way. These assessments provide objective measures of candidates' abilities and help identify top performers in technical tasks.

## REAL-WORLD EXAMPLES:

Coding assessment platforms like HackerRank (www.hackerrank.com) and Codility (www.codility.com) allow companies to administer coding challenges and assessments to evaluate candidates' programming skills and problem-solving abilities.

## TEST PROCTORING

Some assessments have test proctoring available to prevent and detect cheating from online candidates. In some cases, AI technology does the proctoring and monitoring, but other organizations use live remote proctors to help prevent cheating. In the past, test proctoring and monitoring were quite expensive, although prices have come down substantially in recent years. AI proctoring is typically much cheaper than live remote proctoring, although it can be tricky to rely on automated monitoring when it comes to accusations of cheating.

If you consider cheating to be a major concern when screening your job applicants, you should be able to find a testing company and platform that has this capability.

## WHAT SHOULD YOU MEASURE IN YOUR ASSESSMENTS?

As I mentioned earlier, I have worked with many different organizations and have analyzed many different jobs over the past few decades. In this process, we typically review existing job materials and job descriptions and conduct job observations and interviews with job experts.

One of the questions that I typically ask the job experts in these organizations is this: *"What does it take for someone to get fired from this job?"* Of course, I have heard many different answers – but many responses are consistent across companies. It is rare for someone to lose their job because they lack the knowledge, skill, or ability to do the job. If these are issues, training or job changes can typically fix the problem. People losing their jobs because of low skill or weak ability levels does happen on occasion, but it is the exception rather than the rule. On the other hand, personality and motivation issues are much more common employee problems.

---

Bad fit in a job typically results from an *unwillingness* to fit in, rather than an *inability* to do the job.

---

As an example, I can cite years of work that I did with operators and maintenance mechanics at various manufacturing plants in the United States. Almost invariably, job experts responded in two ways when I asked the question of what it takes for someone to lose their job. First, is a lack of safety orientation and violations of safety rules on the job. This seems to be the quickest way for someone to lose their job. And second, poor teamwork behavior is another common reason that people lose their jobs. Very rarely will they cite examples of people losing their jobs because they cannot learn the key skills or lack the knowledge to do the job.

As a result, I strongly recommend that companies assess the *entire applicant* profile when evaluating job candidates and making hiring decisions. Both skills/abilities and personality/motivations should be factored in when deciding whom to hire. Although traditional knowledge and skill tests should be used to identify who is initially qualified for most jobs, bad hires often occur when the personalities and motivations of individuals clash with the organizational culture and personalities of corporate leadership. Because of this, ways of measuring personality and motivation must be part of the applicant screening process. In short, the *whole person* should be evaluated when considering candidates.

As a hiring manager, you should be sure to address this question:

- *What non-cognitive factors would be most effective for screening applicants for key roles in your organization?*

If you are not including these factors in your assessment process, you might want to add validated assessments of these things.

## ENSURING THE VALIDITY OF ASSESSMENTS AND SCREENING TOOLS

As I mentioned at the beginning of this book, I wrote this book to help you understand the reality of hiring processes and where many companies make mistakes. But I have special expertise in employment assessments, and on this topic, I am going to state some facts that are a bit provocative. I say this because I have been in the industry and have this knowledge. It bothers me when most people do not know reality and facts, but we cannot be afraid of it. So here goes:

---

Many assessments that companies use to screen job applicants do not have evidence that they predict job performance.

---

This is <u>not</u> to say that most assessments are completely useless – it's just that they have not demonstrated that they are useful. As a hiring manager and a consumer of assessments used in the applicant screening process, it is okay (and even advisable) for you to ask your HR department or test vendor for this evidence of usefulness. For those of us in organizational psychology, we take this type of evidence seriously and focus on assessment validity (i.e., job relevance); this is our specialty. **Good assessments should have evidence that they are valid!**

This thought process is how the scientific process works. You start by assuming that your intervention (in these cases, the assessment) is <u>in</u>effective. You need to see <u>proof</u> to change your assumption and conclude that it is effective.

It does not work the other way around, where we assume something works until we get proof that it does not work; that would be cheating the scientific method. This proof of test relevance can come from validation studies, which can take different forms, including statistical validity, job content validity, or other creative ways of clearly demonstrating that an assessment is job-related[2].

## WAYS OF OBTAINING VALIDITY EVIDENCE

*Content Validity.* One common way to show that a skill assessment is valid is to ensure that it overlaps with tasks and duties that are done on the job. This is known as job content validity. It requires good documentation of the important tasks and duties that are done on the job; this should be collected in a job analysis. The key aspect of this process is the linkage between test sections (or interview questions) and job tasks. It is not good enough to say that the test *looks like* the job. You need to find a level of specificity to show that each part of the test or interview represents something real that is done on the job.

For example, I remember reviewing a knowledge test for plumbers for a company that wanted to expand its plumbing business. On its face, it seemed easy enough. When I looked at the test, it looked like it covered plumbing stuff. But here's the thing, I did not know plumbing. When I reviewed the job analysis, I did not see much overlap with the test content. And when I gave it to some actual job experts, they pointed out how much of the test covered things that they did not do in that company. And it failed to cover the key things that they were responsible for. So, this test looked OK to me, but it lacked content validity.

*Poor Content Validity – Weak Overlap of Test and Job Content*

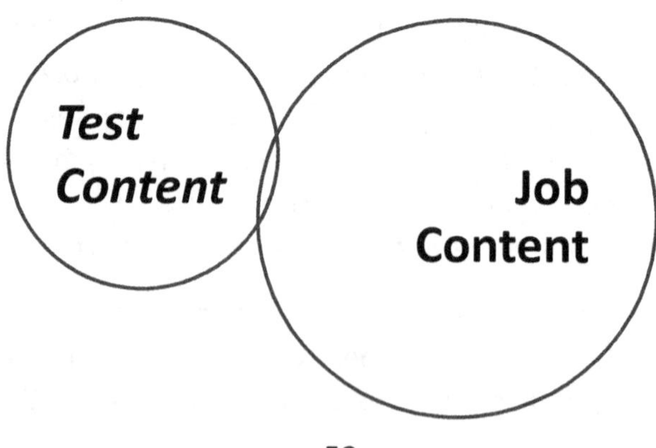

*Good Content Validity – Strong Overlap of Test and Job Content*

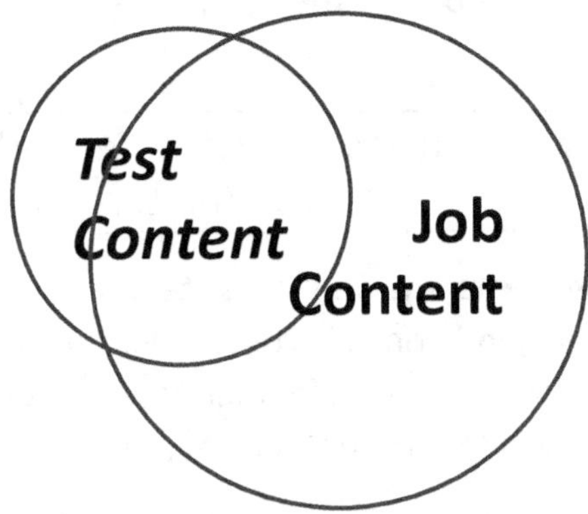


Note that a content validation approach will not work for some ability and personality assessments, as these broad assessments are not usually designed to mirror work that is done on the job. For example, a personality item that measures *conscientiousness* – a trait that many organizations use when screening applicants – might be "I keep my bedroom clean." This would be one reasonable item for measuring conscientiousness, but it is not directly job-relevant. In these cases of assessments that use items and ways of measuring that focus on non-work things, you need to rely on another validation approach.

*Statistical Validity.* When I was in HR consulting, I conducted dozens of statistical validation studies, which were designed to show if assessment results are correlated with job performance. In other words, these studies can demonstrate if better performers on the assessments tend to be better performers on the job. Most of these studies were what we refer to as *concurrent* validation studies, as the assessment data and the criterion (job performance) data are collected at the same time with a group of job incumbents (usually one hundred or more incumbents). So, we would get the group of job incumbents to take the assessment and then get supervisors to rate their level of job performance. The test would demonstrate its validity if we found statistically significant correlations between assessment scores and job performance ratings.

As an example, my previous company had a set of tests that consistently showed good validity for maintenance jobs in manufacturing environments. We ran statistical validity studies of these assessments in similar jobs for a bunch of different companies, and the results of the validity studies were quite consistent. Each time, we were able to show that employees who performed well on the tests also performed well on the job. And the results were all statistically significant. **Valid!**

---

Statistical validity studies show if better performers on the test are also better performers on the job.

---

Note that these tests showed consistent validity because they were carefully developed using good principles of test design. In addition, they focused on skills and traits that were important for maintenance jobs. Despite being good tests, they would not be valid for other types of jobs.

However, when validating different assessments, I can cite other examples where things did not go well. I participated in one such project using a different assessment in another job. For this project, the assessment was used in the hiring process, but the collection of validity evidence for the assessment was delayed. Specifically, the organization began using the assessment to screen applicants, and then (after a few years) they asked us to analyze the data to see if the assessment correlated with job performance. So, the test data came from real applicants, and job performance data came from those applicants who were hired (again, a few years after they took the assessment). This is what we call a *predictive* validation study. Astute readers will understand that only the applicants with higher scores were hired, and therefore we had a "range restriction" issue, but we were able to deal with it via proper statistical analyses.

Well, in this case, the assessment results showed zero correlation with all the important job metrics that we could access – including multiple measures of job performance. We also looked to see if higher performers on the assessment tended to stay longer in the organization – again, nothing. So, we were stuck. The company was using the assessment to help screen applicants, but we could not show that it was a valid measure. My best advice in this case was for them to consider an alternative assessment that would be valid. However, it would require a separate study to demonstrate test validity.

WHAT SHOULD YOU DO IN THE CASE OF POOR VALIDITY RESULTS?

If your statistical validation efforts fail to support the relevance and usefulness of the tests, there are some steps to follow. First, you should consider the different ways that you might evaluate whether someone is a good hire. Our standard method for most statistical validation studies is to have supervisors rate job performance. These ratings can be done rigorously and should be completed separately for the validation study.

I recommend using separate performance evaluations because supervisor ratings of job performance that are completed for the organization's performance evaluation process are often limited metrics of job performance. For example, if overall performance is measured on a five-point scale, employees in most companies receive a 3, 4, or 5; 1 and 2 are very rarely used. Because of this, we try to get ratings of job performance that are made for the validation study and are not used for any other purpose. When we collect performance ratings solely for a validation study, we see that supervisors often provide a greater range of ratings.

In addition, good objective measures of job performance are available for some jobs, which can be used for validation. These will likely overlap with supervisor ratings but will be different in some important ways. For instance, objective sales measures are often available for salespeople and can be used as performance metrics. Accordingly, you might be able to use this for the statistical validation study. Customer service representatives also often have objective measures of various relevant parts of their job. As I have seen, these objective measures tend to correlate with supervisor ratings of job performance but are not the same. Therefore, you find somewhat different validation results if you change the performance measures.

Further, there are many ways of running the statistical analysis that should be tried before concluding that an assessment has no validity. Sophisticated data analysts should understand these issues and might find ways to correct artifacts that obscure a real relationship between test and job performance.

But if all available evidence shows that you do not have a valid assessment, you are best advised to find a different test that is valid. The most straightforward way of demonstrating validity is using a content validity approach for a knowledge or skill test. If you develop a test to match the job content, you are sure to find good content validity.

## Brief Review of US Legal and Regulatory Guidelines for Hiring Tests

In the United States, important legal and regulatory guidelines govern the use of hiring tests to ensure fairness, equal opportunity, and compliance with laws. On the topic of fairness and discrimination, companies need to treat their applicants similarly across all demographics and other protected groups (such as race, gender, or ethnicity). Therefore, rules for who gets tested in the hiring process and how the results are used need to be clearly documented and consistently followed.

Beyond that, another key consideration for employers is the concept of *disparate impact*, which refers to the unintentional discrimination that can occur when a seemingly neutral employment practice, such as a hiring test, disproportionately excludes members of a protected group. Unfortunately, disparate impact is fairly common with some types of applicant tests. To reduce the legal and regulatory risk of disparate impact, employers must ensure that hiring tests are necessary and job-relevant.

The Equal Employment Opportunity Commission (EEOC) provides guidelines for employers on the lawful use of hiring tests under Title VII of the Civil Rights Act of 1964. According to the EEOC, employers must demonstrate that hiring tests are job-related and consistent with business necessity, meaning that the tests measure the skills, abilities, or other qualifications necessary for successful job performance.

To comply with legal and regulatory guidelines, employers should carefully evaluate the content, format, and administration of hiring tests to ensure that they are free from bias and discriminatory effects. This may involve conducting validation studies (see section above) to establish the job relevance of the tests, as well as providing accommodations for candidates with disabilities or other impairments that may affect their performance on the tests. Employers should also be sure to train personnel who administer and score the tests to ensure consistency and fairness in the process.

In addition to federal laws and regulations, employers must also consider state and local laws governing the use of hiring tests, which may vary in their requirements and standards. Some states have their own anti-discrimination laws and regulations that impose additional requirements or restrictions on the use of hiring tests, particularly regarding disparate impact analyses. Also, state and local laws are currently being written and implemented regarding the use of AI in testing.

See the Appendix for a further review of the relevant legal and regulatory guidelines for employment testing in the U.S. (page 123) and in non-U.S. countries (page 127).

---

## CHAPTER SUMMARY

It is common for organizations to use various types of standardized assessments in the hiring process for jobs with relatively high-volume hiring. These include skills, abilities, and personality testing. These are important parts of the skills-first hiring approach. However, many companies are using assessments that lack good validity evidence. Even though these assessments are being used consistently, they might not be effective in determining who are the best candidates. Therefore, it is important to consider validity evidence for these assessments, which will help you ensure that the tests are doing their jobs, as well as helping you stay within the boundaries of laws and best practices.

---

FOR MORE INFORMATION

1. Hickman, L., Bosch, N., Ng, V., Saef, R., Tay, L., & Woo, S. E. (2022). Automated video interview personality assessments: Reliability, validity, and generalizability investigations. *Journal of Applied Psychology, 107*(8), 1323–1351. https://doi.org/10.1037/apl0000695

2. Best Practices for Assessment Validation – *Principles for the Validation and Use of Personnel Selection Procedures*: https://www.apa.org/ed/accreditation/personnel-selection-procedures.pdf

*Hiring the right people takes time, the right questions, and a healthy dose of curiosity.*

Richard Branson

# CHAPTER 6

# CONDUCTING EFFECTIVE INTERVIEWS

- The Importance of a Structured Interview Approach

- Choosing the Best Interview Questions

- Using Interviews to Evaluate Soft Skills and Non-Technical Aspects

## What the Hiring Manager Needs to Remember

As a hiring manager, you might be able to leverage your talent acquisition team to complete many steps of the hiring process. However, you will almost certainly be involved at the interview stage. This will allow you to get a lot of good information about your final candidates. But you need to use a structured interview process. Using this type of process, you ask the same questions and evaluate the responses in a standard way, and it will almost always give you more accurate results than unstructured interviews. As part of this process, you should go through interviewer training. Even though more training might not seem worthwhile, I assure you that good training on the interview process will be time well spent.

Mark A. Smith, Ph.D.

L et's get to the interview phase of the hiring process! With just a handful of candidates left in the running, it's time to hone in on finding the perfect fit for your role. Interviews are your chance to dig deeper into a candidate's qualifications, skills, and overall fit for your organization. But here's the secret: planning and structure are the keys to a good interview. Interviews that lack these things might be good for getting to know a person, but they are poor ways of evaluating potential hires.

In this chapter, we'll dive into the power of structured interviews, unpacking how they can help you make informed decisions. Plus, we'll share strategies for crafting the best interview questions and tips for assessing those elusive soft skills and other non-technical aspects of candidates.

## THE IMPORTANCE OF A STRUCTURED INTERVIEW APPROACH

A structured interview involves asking each candidate a standardized set of questions designed to assess specific skills and competencies relevant to the role. Unlike unstructured interviews, which usually lack consistency and objectivity, structured interviews provide a systematic framework for evaluating candidates based on predetermined criteria. This approach helps minimize bias, ensure fairness, and enhance the reliability and validity of the interview process.

Research from organizational psychology has shown that structured interviews can be good predictors of future job performance – but unstructured interviews are poor predictors[1]. And very recent studies have shown that structured interviews (if done well) can have better predictive validity than such things as cognitive ability tests[2].

### INTERVIEWER TRAINING

To help maintain consistency across interviews and candidates, I strongly advocate for the use of interviewer training to help ensure compliance with the planned interview structure. Interviewer training ensures that all interviewers are equipped with the skills and knowledge to conduct interviews consistently and fairly. By providing standardized training on interview techniques, evaluation criteria, and strategies to minimize bias, companies can improve their interview effectiveness and ensure a level playing field for all candidates.

Note that interviewer training should involve practice with the actual interview materials. This type of practice allows interviewers to become comfortable with the questions and evaluation methods that they will use during their interviews. In my experience, general interviewer training is a good start, but adding practice makes it better. And if you can give your interviewers coaching and feedback while they practice their interviewing skills, your training can be great.

Also in my experience, I have seen many managers and members of organizations push back against additional training. However, I think that interviewer training is time well spent, as using a structured interview approach is not natural for most people. I have conducted many of these training courses and have seen that many hiring managers conduct poor interviews before training. This includes asking inappropriate questions and using inconsistent scoring methods – topics that are addressed in the structured interview training.

## EVALUATING AND SCORING INTERVIEW RESPONSES

Structured interviews should rely on scoring rubrics, also called evaluation criteria or interview response matrices, to help interviewers evaluate candidates consistently.

### LIKERT SCALES

Some companies have their interviewers evaluate candidate responses using Likert scales. These involve rating candidates on a scale (e.g., from 1 to 5) for various competencies or attributes. Interviewers assign scores based on the extent to which candidates demonstrate each competency or attribute. In my experience, these are effective for creating numeric scores for candidate evaluation and are easy to use. However, simply using Likert scales leads to limited consistency and low reliability across interviewers.

### BEHAVIORAL ANCHORED RATING SCALES (BARS):

**I recommend using Behavioral Anchored Rating Scales (BARS)** or rating scales with behavioral examples that help evaluate and score interview responses. These scales involve specific behavioral indicators for each level of competency or skill being assessed. In other words, these scales provide examples of good responses, average responses, and poor interview responses. Using this information, interviewers then rate candidates on a scale based on the extent to which they demonstrate these behaviors during the interview. Compared with simple Likert scales, BARS show much better reliability across interviewers, although they take more effort to create.

*Example Interview Evaluation Guidelines: Communication Skills*

| 1 – Poor | 2 | 3 – Competent | 4 | 5 – Exceptional |
|---|---|---|---|---|
| Candidate struggles to articulate their ideas clearly, resulting in confusion among the audience. | | Candidate demonstrates basic verbal communication skills by delivering the message clearly and coherently. | | Candidate exhibits exceptional verbal communication skills by articulating complex ideas with clarity and precision, ensuring understanding among individuals with varying levels of knowledge or cultural backgrounds. |
| They fail to adapt their communication style to accommodate diverse backgrounds or levels of understanding, leading to misinterpretation or misunderstanding of the message. | | They may struggle to effectively tailor their communication at times; for example, in diverse audiences, resulting in some individuals feeling excluded or misunderstood. | | In difficult conversations, they approach conflicts with empathy and diplomacy, actively listening to others' perspectives and finding mutually beneficial solutions. |
| In sensitive or difficult conversations, candidate may avoid addressing conflicts directly, leading to unresolved issues or strained relationships. | | In challenging conversations, candidate addresses conflicts but may lack finesse in navigating disagreements or managing resistance from others. | | Candidate adeptly adapts their communication style to build rapport and establish trust with stakeholders, fostering alignment and achieving desired outcomes even in challenging situations. |

## CHOOSING THE BEST INTERVIEW QUESTIONS

As part of the structured interview process, using a consistent and appropriate set of interview questions is important. As such, selecting the right interview questions is critical to the success of a structured interview.

When choosing questions, consider the following factors:

- *Relevance to the Role:* Tailor questions to assess the skills, experience, and qualifications required for the position. Focus on eliciting information that is directly relevant to the job responsibilities and requirements.

- *Behavioral-Based Questions:* Use mostly behavioral-based questions to explore candidates' past experiences and behaviors in specific situations. These questions typically begin with phrases such as "Tell me about a time when..." or "Give me an example of..." Companies like Amazon and Google are known for using behavioral interview techniques to evaluate candidates' competencies and cultural fit, often asking questions that delve into specific examples of past experiences.

- *Open-Ended vs. Closed-Ended Questions:* You can use a mix of open-ended and closed-ended questions to encourage candidates to provide detailed responses while also allowing for clarification and follow-up. However, <u>you should emphasize the open-ended questions</u> which are the ones that will provide the most useful information. As a result, including common prompts in the interview materials to help interviewers get relevant information from candidates on these open-ended questions is a good idea.

- *Diversity and Inclusion:* Ensure that the wording of interview questions is inclusive and free from bias. Avoid questions that may inadvertently discriminate against candidates based on protected characteristics such as race, gender, age, religion, or disability.

*Examples of Structured Interview Questions for Technical Skills*

| |
|---|
| 1. Can you walk me through a recent project you worked on that required [specific technical skill]? |
| 2. Describe a challenging technical problem you encountered and how you resolved it. |
| 3. Can you explain [specific technical concept] in simple terms? |
| 4. How do you stay updated with the latest trends and advancements in [specific technical field]? |
| 5. What programming languages/tools are you most proficient in, and can you give an example of how you've used them in a previous project? |
| 6. Describe a time when you had to learn a new technical skill quickly. How did you go about it? |

Many companies that use structured interviews for a variety of different jobs find that they need a simple way of organizing them to ensure that the right interview questions are asked for each role. Specifically, they find that using an interview guide database helps their managers use the right competencies and questions for their open roles (example: Quintela - https://quintela.io/).

## ASKING GOOD FOLLOW-UP QUESTIONS

One criticism that I often hear from hiring managers about structured interviews is the lack of deep information that some candidates provide. That is, some candidates often provide only short answers to the interview questions. More talkative candidates might respond with a high level of detail, but many other candidates will give very limited information. In general, the lack of detail from some candidates can be fixed by having planned follow-up questions listed in the interview materials which are designed to draw out the right type and level of information.

Many organizations encourage their interviewers to use the *STAR* model for asking follow-up questions to behavioral interview questions. In this method, interviewers help to guide candidate

responses to behavioral questions ("Tell me about a time when...") by asking them more information about the <u>S</u>ituation, <u>T</u>ask, <u>A</u>ction, and <u>R</u>esult. Questions that follow this model can help candidates provide details that are most important and can help interviewers assess the relevance of the situation, the effectiveness of the candidate's actions, and the outcomes achieved. In addition, I have found that many candidates have heard of this model during interview prep courses, so they are often ready to provide this type of information.

## USING INTERVIEWS TO EVALUATE SOFT SKILLS AND NON-TECHNICAL ASPECTS

In addition to technical knowledge and expertise, interviews provide an opportunity to evaluate candidates' soft skills and other non-technical traits, such as communication, teamwork, and cultural fit. As you consider these factors as part of the evaluation process, it is again important to remember that the most important aspect of a structured interview is the *consistency* of approach. Therefore, you need to evaluate these non-technical aspects consistently and fairly across individuals. The methods for evaluating these factors should be covered in interviewer training and included in the scoring guidelines.

Consider the following best practices for evaluating these qualities:

- *Behavioral Observations:* Pay attention to candidates' demeanor, body language, and communication style during the interview. Look for evidence of effective communication, active listening, and interpersonal skills.

- *Scenario-Based Questions:* Pose hypothetical scenarios or challenges relevant to the role and observe how candidates respond. Assess their problem-solving abilities, decision-making skills, and adaptability in different situations. Often, these types of questions can be answered even by candidates who lack the experience that is necessary to answer behavioral-based interview questions.

- *Culture Fit:* Evaluate candidates' alignment with the organization's values, mission, and culture. Ask questions that probe candidates' motivations, career goals, and expectations to assess their fit within the team and organization.

*Examples of Structured Interview Questions for "Soft" or Non-Technical Skills*

| | |
|---|---|
| 1. | Can you tell me about a time when you had to work under pressure to meet a tight deadline? How did you handle it? |
| 2. | Describe a situation where you had to resolve a conflict within a team. What approach did you take, and what was the outcome? |
| 3. | Can you give an example of a time when you had to adapt to a significant change at work? How did you approach it? |
| 4. | How do you handle multitasking and managing competing priorities in a fast-paced work environment? |
| 5. | Describe a time when you explained something complicated to someone who didn't know much about it. How did you make it easy to understand? |
| 6. | Tell me about a time when you had to take the initiative to solve a problem or improve a process at work. |

# PANEL OR INDIVIDUAL INTERVIEWS?

Panel interviews (using two or more interviewers with a single candidate) and individual interviews are both common approaches used by employers when evaluating job applicants. Each method carries its own set of advantages and disadvantages, catering to different organizational needs and preferences. I do not have a specific recommendation for one type of interview or the other, so you should consider the benefits and drawbacks of each type of interview.

## PROS AND CONS OF PANEL INTERVIEWS

PROS:

1. *Comprehensive Evaluation*: Panel interviews typically involve multiple interviewers from different departments or levels within the organization. This diversity allows for a comprehensive evaluation of the

candidate's suitability for the role, considering the various perspectives and skillsets required.

2. *Time Efficiency*: Panel interviews can be more time-efficient compared to individual interviews, as they allow for the simultaneous assessment of candidates. This is particularly helpful when screening a large pool of applicants for a single role, streamlining the hiring process.

CONS:

1. *Intimidating Atmosphere*: Facing multiple interviewers at the same time can be intimidating for many candidates, leading to increased stress levels and potentially affecting their performance. This may result in candidates not being able to showcase their true skills and abilities accurately.

2. *Lack of Personalization*: Panel interviews tend to lack the personal touch that individual interviews offer. Candidates might not feel as comfortable or be able to establish rapport with the interviewers, which could impact their overall experience and perception of the company.

## PROS AND CONS OF INDIVIDUAL INTERVIEWS:

PROS:

1. *Personal Connection*: Individual interviews provide an opportunity for a more personalized interaction between the candidate and the interviewer. This allows for a deeper exploration of the candidate's background, experiences, and aspirations, fostering a stronger connection and understanding. Developing this personal connection can be particularly important when there are very few interested candidates for the role.

2. *Tailored Assessment*: In individual interviews, the focus remains solely on the candidate, allowing for a tailored assessment of their skills, qualifications, and cultural fit within the organization. This personalized approach can lead to more insightful evaluations and hiring decisions.

3. *Reduced Pressure*: Candidates may feel less pressure in individual interviews compared to panel interviews because they are conducted in a one-on-one setting. This can create a more relaxed atmosphere, enabling candidates to express themselves more confidently and authentically.

CONS:

1. *Limited Perspectives*: Individual interviews involve only one interviewer, which may result in a narrower range of perspectives and insights compared to panel interviews. This could potentially lead to biases or oversights in the evaluation process.

2. *Time-Consuming*: Conducting individual interviews for each candidate can be more time-consuming compared to panel interviews, especially when screening many applicants. This could prolong the hiring process and cause the organization to expend more resources.

---

## CHAPTER SUMMARY

Conducting effective interviews is important for the validity and integrity of the hiring process. It requires a structured approach, thoughtful selection of relevant interview questions, careful evaluation of both technical and non-technical aspects of candidates, and standardized ways of evaluating candidate responses. By implementing these strategies and using best practices, hiring managers can make informed hiring decisions that lead to successful outcomes for both candidates and organizations.

---

## FOR MORE INFORMATION


1. Campion, M. A., Palmer, D. K., & Campion, J. E. (1997). A Review of Structure in the Selection Interview. *Personnel Psychology*, 50, 655–702. https://doi.org/doi.org/10.1111/j.1744-6570.1997.tb00709.

2. Sackett, P. R., Zhang, C., Berry, C. M., & Lievens, F. (2022). Revisiting meta-analytic estimates of validity in personnel selection: Addressing systematic overcorrection for restriction of range. *Journal of Applied Psychology*, 107(11), 2040–2068. https://doi.org/10.1037/apl0000994

75

*People are not your most important asset. The right people are.*

Jim Collins (author)

# CHAPTER 7

# MAKING THE HIRING DECISION

- Collaborative Decision-Making: Involving Stakeholders

- Balancing Skills with Culture Fit

- What Happens When You Cannot Make the Final Hiring Decision?

**What the Hiring Manager Needs to Remember**

Up to this point in the hiring process, there have been various steps designed to determine which of many candidates should be dropped from consideration for the role. But at some point, a small number of final candidates is determined. And often, they will all be well qualified for the open role. It is commonly accepted that you should use your judgment to select the person you are most comfortable with. However, simply using "gut feel" is potentially problematic and could lead to biased decisions. By following best practices, you should be able to make your final decision confidently while being able to explain why you made your final choice.

Welcome to the home stretch of the hiring process! As you approach the final decision, the pressure is on you to make the right call. Sometimes, it's clear-cut — there's one standout candidate who's a perfect fit. But what about when you're torn between several equally qualified contenders?

In this chapter, we'll tackle the challenge of making that final hiring decision head-on. If you're feeling uncertain or overwhelmed, fear not — we've got you covered with strategies to gather the information you need to make a confident choice. Plus, we'll delve into the key considerations and savvy tactics that you should use to identify the best candidate among the finalists. In particular, I encourage you to use information from multiple sources, rather than just the final interviews.

## COLLABORATIVE DECISION-MAKING: INVOLVING STAKEHOLDERS

Although it is your choice, I recommend involving other stakeholders in the final hiring decision. They can provide valuable insights, offer diverse perspectives, and allow buy-in from team members who are not making the hiring decision.

Consider the following approaches for collaborative decision-making:

- *Gather Cross-Functional Input:* Seek input from various stakeholders, including team members, department heads, and senior leadership, to ensure a comprehensive assessment of each candidate's fit for the role and the organization. As much as possible, ask for descriptive information about the candidates more than a simple hire / not-hire recommendation.

- *Review Interview Notes and Feedback:* Multiple stakeholders may have had the opportunity to participate in the interview process and collectively evaluate candidates based on predetermined criteria and job requirements. Check to see if there are important pieces of feedback that should be used to determine the best hire for the team.

- *Find a Consensus:* Schedule a quick meeting and facilitate open discussions among stakeholders to reach a consensus on the best candidate for the role. Encourage transparency, active listening, and constructive feedback to ensure alignment and agreement on the final decision.

## BALANCING SKILLS WITH CULTURE FIT

Balancing an evaluation of ability and skills with culture fit is essential for finding a candidate who not only possesses the necessary technical ability but also aligns with the organization's values, mission, and culture.

Consider these factors when evaluating fit:

- *Values Alignment:* Assess candidate alignment with the organization's core values, beliefs, and principles. Look for candidates who demonstrate behaviors and attitudes that resonate with the company culture and would contribute positively to the work environment.

- *Team Dynamics:* Consider how each candidate's personality, communication style, and working preferences will complement the existing team dynamics and contribute to a cohesive and collaborative work environment.

- *Organizational Fit:* Evaluate candidates' fit within the broader organizational context, considering factors such as interpersonal style, decision-making style, and organization structure. Seek candidates who can adapt and thrive within the organization's unique culture and ecosystem.

This information can come from candidate interviews, as well as assessment results and other sources. Be sure to consider all relevant information.

## SHOULD YOU USE REFERENCES AND BACKGROUND CHECKS?

Before making their hiring decisions, some organizations conduct reference and background checks to verify candidates' qualifications, experiences, and suitability for the role. Although I do not consider these checks to be necessary for every job, you should consider whether this is appropriate for your role. If it is relevant to your open job, here are some methods and types of information for you to consider:

- *Reference Checks:* Reach out to previous employers, colleagues, or professional contacts provided by the candidates to gather insights into their performance, work ethic, and character. Although many companies have rules against providing much information, you might have the opportunity to ask specific questions to individuals from organizations who are willing to provide feedback about the candidate's skills, work style, and areas for development.

- *Background Checks:* Conduct background checks to verify candidates' education, employment history, credentials, and any criminal or legal records. Be sure to check with your legal team to ensure compliance with applicable laws and regulations governing background screening practices. However, for most roles, I recommend that you <u>not</u> completely rule out someone because of a previous criminal history (assuming it is a nonviolent offense).

- *Due Diligence:* Review the information gathered from reference and background checks carefully, paying attention to any red flags or discrepancies that may warrant further investigation or clarification. Use this information to make an informed and confident hiring decision.

## WHAT HAPPENS WHEN YOU CANNOT MAKE THE FINAL HIRING DECISION?

When you are faced with multiple final candidates who are similarly qualified and input from other stakeholders is inconclusive, making the final hiring decision can be challenging. In such situations, you should carefully consider various factors and employ additional strategies to determine the best candidate for the role. This step might include a look at other factors that you did not consider previously.

Here are some approaches to help you make this decision:

## ASK FOR ADDITIONAL INTERNAL FEEDBACK

Encourage stakeholders who interacted with the candidates to provide additional examples or anecdotes that highlight each candidate's strengths, weaknesses, and potential impact on the team or organization. While individual opinions may be inconclusive, collective input from multiple stakeholders can help identify nuances and considerations that you might not have noticed.

## SEEK OUTSIDE INPUT

Engage in further discussions with trusted external consultants or other individuals, including team members, colleagues, and senior leadership, to gather additional perspectives and insights. Discussions with these additional people who have not interacted with the final candidates are often useful if they ask good questions and prompt thinking from you that you would not have engaged in alone.

## CONDUCT ADDITIONAL IN-DEPTH ASSESSMENTS

Consider conducting additional assessments or exercises to further evaluate the candidates' skills, competencies, and fit for the role. This could include job simulations, case studies, or role-playing exercises designed to assess specific job-related competencies. If used at this point in the process, I recommend using more rigorous assessments than ones from earlier in the hiring process. If there are multiple in-depth assessments and role-play exercises with expert assessors, companies often refer to this step as an "assessment center." These additional assessments can provide deeper insights into how candidates perform in real-world scenarios and help differentiate between closely matched candidates.

---

Interactive assessments using human assessors can provide deep and important information for making a final hiring decision.

---

Note that role-play exercises and other intensive assessments can be more time-consuming and costly than assessments used earlier in the process.

However, you will not need to conduct many of them when you are down to the final two or three candidates. When used appropriately at this late stage, these assessments can provide valuable information to crystallize your hiring decision. They can also provide important information about the person whom you hire that can be used in the onboarding and professional development process.

## Utilize Relevant Objective Criteria

Employ objective criteria to evaluate candidates based on <u>relevant</u> metrics that are strong indicators of skill levels. This could include criteria such as work projects, credentials, certifications, technical skills, or demonstrated achievements. By objectively assessing each candidate against predetermined criteria, you can make a more informed and data-driven decision. However, in keeping with the skills-first approach to hiring, I recommend not weighing education degrees or years of experience too heavily.

## Consider Future Potential

Assess each candidate's potential for growth, development, and long-term success within the organization. Consider factors such as career aspirations, willingness to learn and adapt, leadership potential, and cultural fit. While candidates may be similarly qualified for the open role, their potential for future contributions and advancement within the organization can be a deciding factor.

However, you should be careful not to fall into the trap of simply hiring younger candidates and claiming it is because of their stronger future potential with the company. This opens you to lawsuits in the U.S. based on the Age Discrimination in Employment Act (ADEA) and is generally a bad practice, as you cannot realistically expect people to stay more than ten years with your company.

## Focus on Fit with Team Dynamics

Evaluate each candidate's fit with the existing team dynamics and culture of the organization. Consider factors such as communication style, collaboration preferences, personality traits, and compatibility with team members. Choose the candidate whose working style aligns best with the team's dynamics and who is likely to integrate seamlessly into the existing team environment.

## CONSIDER A TRIAL PERIOD

In some situations, you might consider offering a trial period or contract-based assignment to final candidates before making a final hiring decision. This allows you to assess their performance, capabilities, and fit within the organization in a real-world context before making a long-term commitment. Although such probationary periods are somewhat rare in most organizations, they can be a useful way to make a hire without an initial long-term commitment.


## SHOULD YOU SIMPLY TRUST YOUR INSTINCTS?

Ultimately, many people will tell you that you just need to trust your instincts and intuition as the hiring manager. They will advise you to remember your gut feelings and impressions from interactions with each candidate throughout the hiring process.

However, I would advocate that you look for clear reasons why you are making your final hiring decisions. If you simply trust your instinct, you might end up relying on your biases or just playing favorites (for example, hiring from your former university). Or you might end up making the same type of hiring decision that you typically make. Further, I recommend that you write a note for yourself that includes your rationale for making this important decision. If you cannot provide this information, then you might not be ready to make this decision.

---

Your hiring decisions should be made based on good evidence, rather than gut feel.

---

## CHAPTER SUMMARY

Making the final hiring decision requires a thoughtful and strategic approach that incorporates collaborative decision-making, consideration of culture fit, and a clear thought process. By involving stakeholders and balancing skills with culture fit, organizations can select the best candidate for the role and set them up for success within the organization. When faced with multiple final candidates who are similarly qualified, you must employ additional strategies to make the final hiring decision. By utilizing relevant objective criteria, considering future potential, seeking additional input, and focusing on fit with team dynamics, you can select the best candidate for the role with confidence. If it is not possible to select one person for the job based on the information collected in the hiring process, there are ways to get more information to make the best decision in an informed way.

*Employee orientation centers around and exists to help the individual employee, but it is the company that ultimately reaps the benefits of this practice.*

Michael Watkins (author)

# CHAPTER 8

# ONBOARDING AND INTEGRATION: SETTING NEW HIRES UP FOR SUCCESS

- The Importance of Onboarding and Integration

- Strategies for Fostering a Positive Onboarding Experience

- Example Onboarding Schedule

| **What the Hiring Manager Needs to Remember** |
|---|

Even though the hiring process is complete when someone is selected and agrees to the job, you should also consider their longer-term success. To do this, you should stay in regular communication with your new hires even before their official start date. You should also make yourself available on their first few workdays to ensure that they feel comfortable and prepared to add value. Even if your company has an orientation process, you will want to check in so they know that you have not forgotten about them and are excited to have them on the team. And finally, you need to be sure that there is a plan for the new employees to stay and grow with the company.

This book would seem incomplete if I failed to address the next phase after hiring – onboarding and integration. While the hiring process may officially end once someone joins the organization, the journey is far from over. Integrating new employees into your company culture can be a lengthy process, but it's essential for their success and satisfaction in the long run.

In this chapter, we'll dive into why effective onboarding is crucial, unpack the key elements of a successful onboarding program, and share strategies for creating a welcoming and supportive environment that sets your new hires up for years of success.

## THE IMPORTANCE OF ONBOARDING AND INTEGRATION

Onboarding goes beyond paperwork and a mere first-day administrative orientation. It encompasses the entire process of integrating new employees into the organization's culture, values, and workflows. A well-designed onboarding program can have numerous benefits for both the organization and the new hire, including:

- *Accelerated Time-to-Productivity:* Effective onboarding programs help new hires ramp up quickly and become productive contributors to the organization's goals and objectives.

- *Improved Retention:* Research shows that employees who experience a positive onboarding process are more likely to stay with the organization long-term, reducing turnover and associated costs[1].

- *Enhanced Engagement:* Onboarding fosters a sense of belonging and connection to the organization, increasing employee engagement, morale, and job satisfaction.

- *Cultural Assimilation:* Onboarding helps new hires understand and embrace the organization's culture, values, and norms, leading to better alignment and integration within the team and broader organization.

# STRATEGIES FOR FOSTERING A POSITIVE ONBOARDING EXPERIENCE

There are several strategies organizations can employ to foster a positive onboarding experience for new hires:

- *Personalized Approach:* Tailor the onboarding experience to the individual needs, preferences, and learning styles of each new hire. Consider their background, experience, and career goals when designing their onboarding journey. Smaller organizations have the natural advantage of being able to offer a more personalized onboarding experience.

- *Welcoming Environment:* Create a warm and welcoming environment for new hires from day one. Ensure that their workspace is clean, organized, and equipped with the necessary tools and resources. Assign a designated point of contact to welcome them, answer questions, and provide support throughout the onboarding process.

- *Clear Expectations:* Set clear expectations and goals for new hires from the outset. Outline performance expectations, key responsibilities, and success metrics to help them understand what is expected of them and how their contributions align with organizational objectives. Ensure that new hires understand not only their own responsibilities but also how their role fits into the broader team and company objectives.

- *Encouragement of Questions:* Encourage new hires to ask questions, seek clarification, and express concerns during the onboarding process. Create a safe and supportive environment where they feel empowered to voice their thoughts and opinions without fear of judgment or reprisal. This is particularly important for smaller companies that typically have more frequent interaction between employees and company leadership.

- *Celebration of Milestones:* Recognize and celebrate important milestones and achievements during the onboarding journey. Whether it's completing training modules, reaching performance targets, or finishing probationary periods, acknowledge and celebrate new hires' progress and accomplishments.

- *Ongoing Support:* Provide ongoing support and resources to new hires beyond the initial onboarding period. Offer opportunities for continued learning and development, mentorship, and career advancement to help them grow and succeed in their roles.


## EXAMPLE ONBOARDING SCHEDULE – WEEK 1 AND BEYOND

To help illustrate how companies are handling onboarding, I present an example onboarding schedule of events that reflects what large companies emphasize during new employee orientation. I understand that this specific schedule is not possible for most companies, but the content and structure are good and might be helpful for you to consider.

### DAY 1: WELCOME AND ORIENTATION

Morning:

- *Welcome Breakfast*: New hires are welcomed with a breakfast or coffee session where they meet their managers, colleagues, and key team members. They receive a warm introduction to the company culture and values.

- *Company Overview*: HR conducts an orientation session to provide an overview of the company's history, mission, vision, and organizational structure. New hires learn about the company's products/services, target market, and competitive landscape.

Afternoon:

- *HR Paperwork*: New hires complete necessary paperwork, including tax forms, benefits enrollment, and company policies acknowledgment.

- *IT Setup*: IT support assists new hires in setting up their workstations, email accounts, and access to company systems.


Evening:

- *Welcome Lunch*: New hires enjoy a casual lunch with their immediate team members, fostering camaraderie and social integration.

## DAY 2: ROLE AND DEPARTMENT DEEP DIVE

Morning:

- *Team Introduction*: New hires meet with their immediate team members to gain insights into team dynamics, roles, and responsibilities. They discuss ongoing projects, goals, and expectations.

- *Manager Check-in*: Managers schedule one-on-one meetings with new hires to check-in and discuss job expectations, goals, and performance metrics.

Afternoon:

- *Department Overview*: New hires attend sessions led by department heads or senior team members to gain a deeper understanding of their department's functions, goals, and key initiatives.

- *Role-specific Training*: New hires participate in role-specific training sessions or workshops tailored to their job responsibilities. They learn about tools, processes, and best practices relevant to their roles.

Evening:

- *Networking Event*: New hires attend a company-sponsored networking event or social gathering, providing opportunities to connect with colleagues from different departments and build relationships.

## DAY 3: COMPANY CULTURE AND VALUES

Morning:

- *Culture Workshop*: HR conducts a workshop to delve into the company's culture, values, and guiding principles. New hires participate in interactive discussions and activities to understand how these values are lived out in everyday work life.

- *Diversity and Inclusion Training*: New hires engage in training sessions focused on fostering diversity, equity, and inclusion in the workplace. They learn about unconscious bias, inclusive communication, and allyship.

Afternoon:
- *Team Building Activity*: New hires participate in a team-building activity or exercise designed to promote collaboration, communication, and trust within their teams.

- *Mentorship Pairing*: New hires are paired with a mentor or buddy who can provide guidance, support, and advice as they navigate their roles and the company culture.

Evening:
- *Social Event*: New hires join a company-sponsored social event, such as a happy hour or team dinner, to further build connections and rapport with colleagues.

## DAY 4: WRAP-UP AND FEEDBACK
Morning:
- *Q&A Session*: New hires have the opportunity to ask questions and seek clarification on any aspects of the onboarding process or company operations.

- *Feedback Session*: HR conducts a feedback session to gather input from new hires about their onboarding experience. This feedback is used to continuously improve the onboarding process.

Afternoon:
- *Goal Setting*: Managers meet with new hires to discuss short-term and long-term goals, expectations, and development opportunities. They collaboratively establish actionable goals and milestones.

- *Follow-up Training*: New hires receive additional training or resources based on their identified learning needs or areas for improvement.

Evening:
- *Welcome Dinner*: The onboarding process concludes with a celebratory dinner or gathering, during which new hires are officially welcomed into the company community and encouraged to contribute their unique perspectives and talents.

This week 1 onboarding schedule combines elements of orientation, training, team integration, and cultural immersion to provide new hires with a comprehensive introduction to the company and set them up for success in their roles. Of course, this schedule goes beyond what most companies – particularly small ones – can do. However, it does show the type of information that is important to cover during initial orientation.

## ONGOING ONBOARDING EVENTS – AFTER WEEK 1

After the initial onboarding week, it is essential to continue supporting new employees as they integrate into the organization and acclimate to their roles. Here are some events or steps that new employees should go through after the first week and throughout the first year of employment:

### ONGOING TRAINING AND DEVELOPMENT

1. *Role-Specific Training:* **Offer** ongoing training sessions or workshops tailored to new employees' roles to deepen their knowledge and skills in specific areas relevant to their job responsibilities.

2. *Professional Development Opportunities:* Provide opportunities for new employees to participate in conferences, webinars, or courses to enhance their professional skills and stay updated on industry trends.

3. *Cross-Functional Training:* Offer opportunities for new employees to gain exposure to different departments or functions within the organization through cross-functional projects, job shadowing, or rotational programs.

### REGULAR CHECK-INS AND FEEDBACK

1. *One-on-One Meetings:* Schedule regular one-on-one meetings between new employees and their managers to provide feedback, address any challenges or concerns, and set goals for continued growth and development.

2. *Performance Reviews:* Conduct periodic performance reviews to evaluate new employees' progress, provide constructive feedback, and recognize achievements. Use these reviews as opportunities to align expectations and identify areas for improvement or further support.

3. *Peer Mentors:* Assign another team member to be the person who answers their questions. These "buddy systems" are now common and provide a good way for new hires to get their questions answered.

4. *Peer Feedback:* Encourage new employees to seek feedback from other peers and colleagues to gain different perspectives, insights, and advice on how to excel in their roles.

SOCIAL AND TEAM-BUILDING ACTIVITIES:
1. *Team Events:* Organize regular team-building activities, social events, or offsite retreats to foster camaraderie, collaboration, and a sense of belonging among team members.

2. *Mentorship Programs:* Pair new employees with mentors or buddies who can provide guidance, support, and advice as they navigate their roles and the organization.

3. *Employee Resource Groups:* Encourage participation in employee resource groups (ERGs) or affinity groups focused on inclusion and professional development to facilitate networking and community-building.

CAREER GROWTH AND ADVANCEMENT:
1. *Career Pathing Discussions:* Have regular conversations with new employees about their career aspirations, interests, and goals. Provide guidance and support to help them identify opportunities for advancement and develop a clear career path within the organization.

2. *Stretch Assignments:* Offer challenging projects or stretch assignments that allow new employees to expand their skills, take on additional responsibilities, and demonstrate their potential for growth and advancement.

3. *Promotion and Recognition:* Recognize and reward new employees for their contributions and achievements through promotions, awards, or

public acknowledgments. Celebrate milestones and successes to reinforce a culture of appreciation and recognition.

By implementing these ongoing events and steps, organizations can ensure that new employees are integrated well into the organization and supported throughout their first year of employment. This not only promotes employee engagement, satisfaction, and retention but also fosters a culture of continuous learning, development, and growth.

## CHAPTER SUMMARY

Onboarding and integration play a crucial role in setting new hires up for success within an organization. By implementing a comprehensive onboarding program that incorporates key components and strategies for fostering a positive experience, organizations can accelerate new hires' time-to-productivity, enhance engagement and retention, and ultimately drive organizational success.

FOR MORE INFORMATION:
1. The Importance of Onboarding: https://www.shrm.org/topics-tools/news/talent-acquisition/dont-underestimate-importance-good-onboarding

*Hiring is the most important people function you have, and most of us aren't as good at it as we think.*

Laszlo Bock (author)

# CHAPTER 9

# OVERCOMING COMMON HIRING PITFALLS

- Addressing Bias in Hiring Decisions

- Learning from Past Mistakes: Case Studies and Examples

---

**What the Hiring Manager Needs to Remember**

As we review the overall hiring process, it is important to bring up some areas where common mistakes occur. In particular, bias is something that has the potential to plague human judgment and should be addressed in an honest and straightforward way. Bias in the hiring process is particularly problematic not only because harms decision-making, but it also can lead to lawsuits in the United States if candidates from protected classes are affected.

---

I t's time to review some of the key challenges and common mistakes that organizations make when hiring new people. Finding the right talent can make or break any organization, and it's no walk in the park. In this chapter, we'll shine a light on some of the common traps that hiring managers like you fall into and share strategies for dodging them.

From tackling biases head-on to learning valuable lessons from other companies, navigating these pitfalls is key to assembling a robust and inclusive team. Get ready to uncover how biases might be sneakily affecting your hiring decisions and discover practical ways to neutralize their impact.

## TYPES OF BIAS IN HIRING

Bias can manifest in various forms throughout the hiring process, influencing decisions and perpetuating inequality. Recognizing and addressing these biases whenever humans make decisions is crucial for creating a fair and inclusive recruitment process. Some common types of bias that occur in the hiring process include:

- *Unconscious Bias:* Unconscious bias refers to various types of hidden attitudes or stereotypes that affect our understanding, actions, and decisions unconsciously. This bias can lead to preferential treatment or discrimination against certain groups based on factors such as race, gender, age, or ethnicity. For example, it seems to be common for hiring managers to unconsciously favor candidates who share similar backgrounds or characteristics to their own, overlooking qualified candidates from other backgrounds.

- *Confirmation Bias:* Confirmation bias occurs when individuals seek out information that confirms their pre-existing beliefs or assumptions while ignoring evidence that contradicts them. In the hiring process, confirmation bias can lead to favoring candidates who align with your initial impressions or expectations, even if they may not be the best fit for the role.

- *Affinity Bias:* Affinity bias involves favoring candidates who share similar interests, backgrounds, or experiences to oneself or the hiring team. This bias can result in you gravitating towards candidates who you might perceive as being more likable or relatable, rather than objectively assessing their qualifications and capabilities.

- *Halo and Horns Effect:* The halo effect occurs when certain positive attributes or qualities of a candidate overshadow any potential weaknesses or shortcomings, leading to an overly favorable evaluation. Conversely, the horns effect occurs when negative attributes or perceptions of a candidate overshadow their positive qualities, resulting in a biased and unfair assessment.

- *Stereotyping:* Stereotyping involves applying generalized assumptions or characteristics to individuals based on their membership in a particular group. Stereotypes can influence hiring decisions by leading to the exclusion of candidates who do not fit into perceived norms or expectations associated with their demographic characteristics.

Addressing bias in the hiring process requires proactive measures such as implementing structured interviews, blind resume screening, training for everyone involved in the hiring process, and regular evaluation of recruitment practices. Companies also attempt to address bias in decision-making during interviewer training. Companies like Microsoft[1] and Facebook[2] offer bias training to employees involved in the hiring process to foster more inclusive practices. By raising awareness of bias and fostering a culture of inclusivity and fairness, organizations can mitigate the impact of bias and create a more equitable hiring process that attracts and retains diverse talent.

In addition, *test bias* is another type of bias that can occur during the hiring process. The other forms of bias that I mentioned involve direct human judgment. However, test bias can affect hiring decisions in different ways when standard tests and assessments are used – even when they are implemented consistently. This type of bias refers to systematic error or unfair advantage from the use of selection tests based on irrelevant factors such as race or gender. This is related to but not the same as disparate impact. Testing experts should be used to evaluate whether test bias is harming your hiring decisions.

## STOPPING BIAS IN HIRING DECISIONS

Bias in hiring decisions can manifest in various forms, including unconscious bias, affinity bias, and confirmation bias. These biases can lead to unfair treatment of candidates and result in missed opportunities for hiring diverse and qualified talent. To address bias in hiring decisions, consider the following strategies:

- *Training and Education:* Provide training and education for hiring managers and recruiters to raise awareness of unconscious bias and its impact on decision-making. Offer workshops, seminars, or online courses that explore topics such as diversity, equity, and inclusion in hiring.

- *Structured Interviewing:* Implement structured interviewing techniques that focus on evaluating candidates based on predetermined criteria and job-related competencies. Use standardized interview questions and evaluation criteria to minimize the influence of bias and ensure fairness and consistency in the hiring process.

- *Diverse Hiring Panels:* Create diverse hiring panels comprising individuals from different backgrounds, perspectives, and experiences. Diverse perspectives can help mitigate bias and promote more inclusive decision-making by challenging assumptions and providing alternative viewpoints. Companies like Airbnb[3] and Pinterest[4] intentionally use diverse hiring panels to include individuals from different backgrounds and perspectives.

- *Blind Screening:* Consider implementing blind screening techniques to remove identifying information such as name, gender, and ethnicity from resumes or applications during the initial screening process. This helps prevent unconscious bias based on demographic factors and allows candidates to be evaluated solely on their qualifications and merits.

- *Data-Driven Decision-Making:* Use data and analytics to track and analyze hiring outcomes, including candidate demographics, selection rates, and retention rates. Identify patterns or trends that may indicate the presence of bias and take proactive measures to address them. Salesforce[5], for example, regularly analyzes hiring data to identify disparities and take targeted actions to promote diversity and inclusion.

## ENSURING ACCESSIBLE HIRING PROCESSES

For both fairness and legal reasons, applicants of all abilities and disability levels need to gain access to job opportunities. There are some steps for companies to take that help ensure that people with disabilities have equal opportunities to succeed in the hiring process requires companies to adopt inclusive practices and provide necessary accommodation. These include:

- *Accessible Application Process*: Make sure that the application process is accessible to candidates with disabilities. This includes having an accessible career website, providing alternative formats for application materials, and offering assistance or accommodations upon request.

- *Transparent Communication*: Clearly communicate the company's commitment to diversity and inclusion, including its support for candidates with disabilities. Provide information about available accommodations and resources and encourage candidates to disclose any accommodations they may need during the hiring process.

- *Flexible Interview Formats*: Offer flexibility in interview formats to accommodate candidates with disabilities. This may include providing options for remote interviews, offering video conferencing platforms with accessibility features, or conducting interviews in accessible locations.

- *Training for Hiring Managers*: Provide training for hiring managers and other interviewers on disability awareness, inclusive hiring practices, and reasonable accommodations. This will ensure that you are familiar with applicable laws and regulations, such as the Americans with Disabilities Act (ADA) and understand their responsibilities in providing accommodations.

- *Other Reasonable Accommodations*: Offer reasonable accommodations to candidates with disabilities to ensure they can fully participate in the hiring process. This may include providing assistive technology, offering additional time for assessments, or adjusting physical environments.

- *Focus on Skills and Abilities*: Evaluate candidates based on their skills, qualifications, and abilities rather than focusing solely on perceived limitations or disabilities. When appropriate, consider alternative ways for candidates to demonstrate their capabilities, such as through skills assessments or work samples.

- *Promote Accessibility in the Workplace*: Create an inclusive and accessible work environment that supports employees with disabilities. This may involve providing ergonomic workstations, ensuring accessible facilities, and offering ongoing support and accommodations as needed.

- *Engage with Disability Organizations*: Partner with disability advocacy organizations and community groups to promote awareness, share best practices, and connect with talented candidates with disabilities. These partnerships can help companies tap into a diverse talent pool and create more inclusive hiring practices.

By implementing these strategies, companies can create a more inclusive and accessible hiring process that enables candidates with disabilities to showcase their talents, skills, and potential contributions to the organization. Embracing diversity and inclusion benefits not only individuals with disabilities but also the entire company, fostering innovation, creativity, and success.

# LEARNING FROM MISTAKES: CASE STUDIES AND EXAMPLES

Learning from past hiring mistakes is essential for improving recruitment processes and making better-informed decisions in the future. And in this case, I would advise you to learn from *others'* mistakes as much as possible. Learning from your own mistakes can be quite painful, at times.

Let's examine some case studies and examples of common hiring pitfalls and the lessons we can glean from them:

## CASE STUDY 1: LACK OF DIVERSITY IN HIRING

*Example:* Company A realized that its workforce lacked diversity, particularly in leadership and other key positions. Upon reflection and analysis, they discovered that their recruitment processes favored candidates from a small number of universities and other specific work backgrounds, resulting in a lack of diversity in these key positions, as well as their talent pipeline.

*Lesson Learned:* Company A expanded its recruiting efforts to different schools and other locations to attract candidates from underrepresented groups. It also implemented bias training for hiring managers and established diversity goals and targets for key positions.

## CASE STUDY 2: IGNORING CULTURAL FIT

*Example:* Company B used a hiring process that focused on recruiting candidates solely based on their technical skills. They did not consider cultural fit in this process. They found that their new hires struggled to adapt to the organization's culture and values, leading to friction with team members and ultimately, a high turnover rate.

*Lesson Learned:* Company B revised its hiring process to include cultural fit as a key consideration at different steps in the hiring funnel. They incorporated behavioral-based interview questions to assess candidates' alignment with the organization's values and conducted panel interviews including team members which focused on evaluating cultural fit from multiple perspectives.

## CASE STUDY 3: POOR CANDIDATE EXPERIENCE

*Example:* During the resume review and applicant assessment steps, Company C failed to communicate effectively with the candidates under consideration. These individuals were unsure of where they stood in the hiring process and were generally frustrated by the recruitment process for this company.

*Lesson Learned:* Company C revised some parts of the hiring process to incorporate candidate updates and a communication portal. They also sent weekly update messages to candidates to ensure that each candidate understood if they were or were not still under consideration for the role. And they worked with hiring managers to make quicker decisions about candidate status.

## CASE STUDY 4: POORLY DEFINED JOB REQUIREMENTS

*Example:* Company D tended to use the same job descriptions for many years. They failed to clearly define the job requirements and qualifications that are necessary for the job. They spent a lot of time responding to calls and requests for more information from unqualified candidates. And they missed out on many potentially suitable ones. This led to increasing time-to-hire over the course of time.

*Lesson Learned:* Company D went back to the start of their hiring process and reviewed the job descriptions and requirements to make sure that they were updated and accurate. This led to several changes – both in adding new factors to these documents, as well as taking away information that was no longer relevant or accurate.

## CHAPTER SUMMARY

Overcoming common hiring pitfalls requires a proactive approach that addresses bias in hiring decisions and incorporates lessons learned from past mistakes. By implementing strategies such as training and education, structured interviewing, diverse hiring panels, blind screening, and data-driven decision-making, organizations can foster more inclusive and effective recruitment processes that lead to better hiring outcomes and a stronger, more diverse workforce.

FOR MORE INFORMATION

1. Microsoft - Diversity and Inclusion: https://careers.microsoft.com/v2/global/en/diversityandinclusion
2. Facebook Diversity and Inclusion: https://www.facebook.com/community/diversity-and-inclusion/
3. Airbnb Diversity & Inclusion: https://www.airbnb.com/resources/hosting-homes/t/diversity-inclusion-41
4. Pinterest Diversity, Equity & Inclusion: https://www.pinterestcareers.com/en/life-at-pinterest-blog/inclusion-diversity/
5. Salesforce Equality: https://www.salesforce.com/company/equality/

*The future depends on
what you do today.*

Mahatma Gandhi

# CHAPTER 10

# THE FUTURE OF HIRING

- Embracing Technology: AI, Automation, and the Metaverse

- Trends in Remote Work and Distributed Teams

- Adapting to Evolving Skill Requirements

---

**What the Hiring Manager Needs to Remember**

Technology, such as AI and virtual reality, has already affected the hiring steps in several prominent organizations. In particular, generative AI has allowed many companies to save a lot of time and effort by using it for various aspects of their hiring processes. As a hiring manager, you need to get on board with this new technology and encourage others in your organization to use it. Not only does it have the potential to save time, but it can also help improve the candidate experience and even make better hiring decisions. These new technologies will likely be used even more in the future, so you might as well get used to them.

---

Welcome to the frontier of hiring! Just as the world of work is constantly evolving, so too is the way we hire. In this chapter, we'll take a glimpse into the crystal ball of hiring trends and technologies that are shaping the future.

From embracing cutting-edge tech and automation to navigating the new normal of remote work and global teams, staying ahead of the curve is crucial for organizations to attract and keep top talent in today's fast-paced world. Get ready to explore the technologies already shaking up the hiring process and what exciting changes the future holds.

## EMBRACING TECHNOLOGY: AI, AUTOMATION, AND THE METAVERSE

Technology is revolutionizing the hiring process, enabling organizations to streamline recruitment, improve efficiency, and make more data-driven decisions. Here are some key technological trends shaping the future of hiring:

- *AI and Machine Learning:* AI-powered tools and algorithms are increasingly being used to screen resumes, assess candidate fit, and predict job performance. In fact, talent acquisition has been one of the first areas within HR that has taken advantage of AI/ML to do their work. Machine learning algorithms can analyze vast amounts of data to identify patterns and trends, helping recruiters make more informed hiring decisions.

- *Automation:* Automation involves transforming repetitive and time-consuming tasks in the hiring process, such as scheduling interviews, sending follow-up emails, and conducting background checks. Automated workflows and chatbots can enhance the candidate experience by providing instant responses to inquiries and speeding up the recruitment process. This technology can be very useful in maintaining communication with job applicants and answering their basic questions.

- *Virtual Reality (VR) and Augmented Reality (AR):* VR and AR technologies are revolutionizing the way organizations assess candidates' skills and competencies. Virtual simulations and interactive experiences allow candidates to showcase their abilities in realistic scenarios, providing recruiters with valuable insights into their capabilities and fit for the role. As VR headsets are becoming more commonplace, organizations are starting to find ways to use them in the talent acquisition process. As an example, Accenture, the global consulting and professional services firm, has already incorporated VR technology into its recruitment process[1].

- *Metaverse:* The metaverse, a virtual shared space created by the convergence of physical and virtual reality, presents new opportunities for recruitment and talent acquisition. Organizations can host virtual career fairs, networking events, and interviews in immersive virtual environments, reaching candidates from around the world and enhancing the recruitment experience. Companies are also starting to use this shared space in their onboarding and orientation processes. For instance, Deloitte has used VR and the metaverse for virtual office tours and onboarding sessions[2].

To take advantage of new technology in the hiring process, I recommend that you find training and other resources to help you understand it. For example, I recently participated in a useful interactive training course on virtual reality and extended reality from Edstutia (https://edstutia.com/). This type of training was important for me because it would have been nearly impossible to understand new technology like VR without experiencing it firsthand. And you will need coaching and individualized instruction to gain a proper appreciation of it.

As much as work has changed over the past decade, it will likely change at an even greater rate in the next decade. Finding the right resources and staying updated will be an ongoing challenge for everyone.

---

AI is not just transforming talent acquisition; it's redefining the very nature of work.

---

# TRENDS IN REMOTE WORK AND DISTRIBUTED TEAMS

The COVID pandemic accelerated the adoption of remote work and distributed teams, transforming the way organizations approach talent acquisition and management. Here are some key trends shaping the future of remote work:

- *Hybrid Work Models:* Many organizations are embracing hybrid work models, allowing employees to split their time between remote and office-based work. This flexible approach accommodates diverse preferences and lifestyles while maintaining collaboration and connectivity within teams.

- *Global Talent Pool:* The potential for remote work has enabled organizations to tap into a global talent pool, accessing top talent regardless of geographical location. This diversity of talent brings fresh perspectives, skills, and experiences to the organization, driving innovation and creativity.

- *Remote Onboarding and Integration:* With remote work becoming the norm, organizations are adapting their onboarding and integration processes to accommodate remote employees. Virtual onboarding sessions, digital welcome kits, and remote team-building activities help new hires feel connected and engaged from day one.

- *Digital Collaboration Tools:* The rise of remote work has led to increased reliance on digital collaboration tools such as video conferencing, project management platforms, and messaging apps. These tools facilitate communication, collaboration, and productivity among distributed teams, enabling seamless remote work experiences.

# ADAPTING TO EVOLVING SKILL REQUIREMENTS

As industries evolve and technology advances, the skills required in the workforce are also changing rapidly. Here are some key strategies for organizations to adapt to evolving skill requirements:

- *Continuous Learning and Development:* Encourage a culture of continuous learning and development within the organization. Provide employees with access to training programs, online courses, and professional development opportunities to acquire new skills and stay competitive in their fields.

- *Upskilling and Reskilling:* Identify emerging skill gaps within your organization and invest in upskilling and reskilling initiatives to address them. Offer training programs and certifications in areas such as digital literacy, data analysis, and technology proficiency to equip employees with the skills needed for the future of work.

- *Flexible Talent Strategies:* Embrace flexible talent strategies such as gig work, freelancing, and project-based hiring to access specialized skills and expertise on demand. Leverage platforms and networks (like UpWork) that connect organizations with independent contractors and freelancers to supplement internal capabilities.

- *Collaboration with Educational Institutions:* Partner with educational institutions, universities, and training providers to develop tailored programs and curricula that align with the evolving skill requirements of the workforce. Foster relationships with academia to bridge the gap between education and employment and ensure that graduates are equipped with the skills needed for the future of work. Remember that junior colleges and community colleges are often the best places for this type of collaboration.

## CHAPTER SUMMARY

The future of hiring is characterized by rapid technological advancements, changing work patterns, and evolving skill requirements. By embracing technology, adapting to remote work trends, and investing in continuous learning and development, organizations can position themselves for success in a dynamic and competitive landscape. By staying ahead of these trends and embracing innovation, organizations can attract, retain, and empower top talent to drive future growth and success.

FOR MORE INFORMATION

1. For information about Accenture: https://www.accenture.com/us-en/careers/explore-careers/area-of-interest/journey-to-accenture
2. For information about Deloitte: https://app.blend.media/blog/deloitte-digital-virtual-recruitment

113

*Time spent on hiring is
time well spent.*


Robert Half (business owner)

# CHAPTER 11

# CONCLUSION AND FINAL RECOMMENDATIONS FOR HIRING MANAGERS

-   Recap of Key Points

-   Encouragement for Implementing the Skills-First Approach

-   Looking Ahead: Continuous Improvement in Hiring Practices

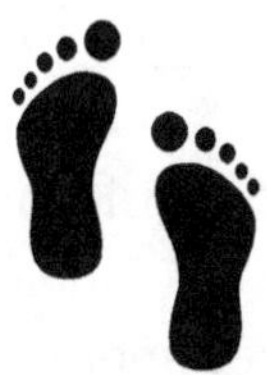

---

**What the Hiring Manager Needs to Remember**

Even though this is a relatively short book, we covered many different issues in the hiring process that are directly relevant for hiring managers. We review each chapter in this final chapter, but mostly we focus on the recommendations for you – the hiring manager.

---

Congratulations on reaching the finish line of this book! As you close these pages, I hope you've gleaned valuable insights into the skills-first hiring approach and the essential aspects of proper talent acquisition. As a manager, your influence on your organization's success through sound hiring decisions is immense.

In this concluding chapter, let's revisit the key lessons we've learned along the way and offer actionable recommendations to fuel your journey toward assembling top-notch teams. Get ready for a quick recap of the gems from each chapter as we wrap up our journey together.

## EMBRACING THE SKILLS-FIRST HIRING APPROACH

In Chapter 2, we explored the fundamental principles of the skills-first hiring approach. This idea emphasizes prioritizing candidates' demonstrated skills and competencies over traditional credentials such as education and years of experience. By focusing on skills, you open doors to a more diverse talent pool and ensure that candidates are directly assessed based on their potential to excel in the role.

*Recommendation*: Embrace the skills-first hiring approach by reevaluating your recruitment processes and job requirements. Look beyond resumes and education level to identify candidates with the right skills and aptitudes to thrive in your organization. In particular, small and mid-sized organizations should find ways to tap into a diverse pool of talent and identify individuals who possess the practical competencies needed to thrive in the role. If you do this, you will be better able to compete with large companies that have more resources.

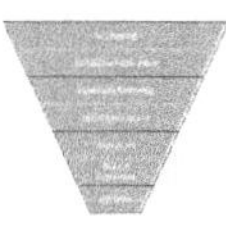

## NAVIGATING THE TALENT ACQUISITION FUNNEL

Chapter 3 introduced the concept of the talent acquisition funnel—a systematic approach to attracting, screening, and selecting candidates. Understanding the stages of the funnel, from sourcing to onboarding, is essential for optimizing your hiring process and maximizing efficiency.

*Recommendation*: Implement a structured talent acquisition process tailored to your organization's needs. Streamline processes, leverage technology, and establish clear metrics to track progress and identify areas for improvement. Smaller companies will often use a less structured hiring approach, and this flexibility can help them make hiring decisions quickly. However, it is still important for you to fully consider a wide range of candidates for your roles.

## DEFINING CORE JOB SKILLS AND WRITING JOB DESCRIPTIONS

In Chapter 4, we discussed the importance of defining core job skills and writing clear, concise job descriptions. A well-crafted job description serves as the foundation for effective recruitment, helping to attract qualified candidates and align expectations between you and the candidates.

*Recommendation*: Collaborate with team members and stakeholders to identify the key skills and competencies required for success in each role. Use this information to craft compelling job descriptions that accurately reflect the demands of the position. Managers in smaller organizations typically have less support for the recruitment process, but you need to be sure that you spend the time and effort early in the process so you understand and can communicate the nature of their open role.

## ASSESSMENT AND SCREENING PROCESS

Chapter 5 delved into the assessment and screening process, highlighting the importance of using validated tools and techniques to evaluate candidates objectively. From skills assessments to behavioral interviews, incorporating a variety of methods ensures a comprehensive evaluation of candidates' suitability for the role.

*Recommendation*: Invest in validated assessment tools to improve the accuracy and reliability of candidate evaluations. Tailor assessments to align with job requirements and organizational values, ensuring a robust screening process. Small and mid-sized organizations often do not have established assessment processes. However, with the computerized nature of today's assessments, it is now practical for you to use applicant assessments.

## CONDUCTING EFFECTIVE INTERVIEWS

In Chapter 6, we explored strategies for conducting effective interviews that elicit valuable insights into candidates' skills, experiences, and motivations. Structured interviews, behavioral questioning techniques, and panel interviews are among the approaches discussed to facilitate fair and thorough candidate assessments.

*Recommendation*: Standardize interview processes and questions to minimize bias and ensure consistency across candidates. Train interviewers to probe for specific examples and assess candidates' alignment with job competencies and cultural fit. Even if you are in a smaller company, you should take steps to ensure that your interviews are completed and evaluated consistently.

## MAKING THE FINAL HIRING DECISION

Chapter 7 addressed the complexities of making the final hiring decision, emphasizing the importance of weighing various factors, including skills, cultural fit, and team dynamics. Collaboration between yourself, HR professionals, and other key stakeholders is essential for making informed hiring decisions that align with organizational goals.

*Recommendation*: Foster open communication and collaboration among decision-makers involved in the hiring process. Leverage data and insights gathered throughout the recruitment process to inform decision-making and take steps to find additional candidate information, if needed. Managers in smaller organizations often find themselves lacking pieces of information and find in-depth assessments in the final stage quite useful in making the final call.

## ONBOARDING AND INTEGRATION: SETTING NEW HIRES UP FOR SUCCESS

In Chapter 8, we discussed the critical role of onboarding and integration in setting new hires up for success. A well-structured onboarding program ensures that new employees feel welcome, supported, and equipped to contribute effectively from day one.

*Recommendation*: Develop a comprehensive onboarding program that addresses both practical and cultural aspects of integration. Assign mentors or buddies to help new hires navigate the organization and provide ongoing support throughout their transition. Small and mid-sized organizations will typically not have a standard orientation process for new hires, but you can take advantage of this by tailoring the process for each new hire to help ensure their long-term success.

## OVERCOMING COMMON HIRING PITFALLS

Chapter 9 examined common hiring pitfalls and challenges that you may encounter, from unconscious bias to inefficient processes. By proactively addressing these pitfalls, you can minimize risks and optimize outcomes throughout the hiring process.

*Recommendation*: Prioritize hiring the most qualified candidates, but pay close attention to diversity, equity, and inclusion in your hiring practices to mitigate bias and promote fairness. Continuously evaluate and refine your recruitment strategies to adapt to changing market dynamics and organizational needs.

## THE FUTURE OF HIRING

In the final chapter, we explored emerging trends and technologies shaping the future of hiring. From AI-powered recruitment tools to virtual reality simulations, staying informed about industry advancements enables you to stay ahead of the curve and leverage innovative solutions to attract and retain top talent.

*Recommendation:* Stay curious and adaptable in your approach to hiring, embracing new technologies and methodologies that enhance your ability to identify and engage with candidates. Foster a culture of continuous learning and improvement to remain competitive in a rapidly evolving landscape. Due to the widely available nature of new technologies, many smaller companies can use AI as effectively as larger ones.

As a hiring manager, you play a pivotal role in shaping the success and growth of your organization. After all, there is no more important decision that you will make than choosing who works for your company. By implementing the principles and recommendations outlined in this book, you can build diverse, high-performing teams that drive innovation, productivity, and organizational excellence. Thank you for joining us on this journey toward transformative hiring practices. Best wishes for your future hiring endeavors!

## FINAL THOUGHT ABOUT SKILLS-FIRST HIRING

I did want to include one more thought about a skills-first hiring approach. It is not anti-education. In fact, a skills-first hiring approach requires a good education system to maximize candidate skills. In most cases, people do not acquire their skills naturally and without help from teachers. So, if it is practical, I encourage people to get an education – often by attending traditional colleges and universities.

But the practical issues of college are real and imposing. Attending a college for four years is a major time commitment. And getting a degree can be very expensive – particularly in the U.S. It is unfair for companies to place these barriers in front of candidates if there are other ways to obtain relevant skills.

Attending universities is not the only path to the skills needed for many jobs. We all have a tremendous amount of access to information at any given moment. If properly directed and motivated, individuals can learn the skills needed for many jobs in much less time and for much less money than the universities charge. This is the reality of our era. No one has a monopoly on knowledge and skills.

---

For many jobs, learning and skills are essential.
College degrees don't need to be.

---

# APPENDICES

1. LEGAL COMPLIANCE FOR HIRING IN U.S.-BASED COMPANIES

2. LEGAL COMPLIANCE FOR HIRING IN COUNTRIES OUTSIDE OF THE UNITED STATES

3. TESTIFYING AS AN EXPERT ON SKILLS-FIRST HIRING TO U.S. HOUSE OF REPRESENTATIVES

4. GLOSSARY OF RECRUITING AND HIRING TERMS

# APPENDIX 1

# LEGAL COMPLIANCE FOR HIRING IN U.S.-BASED COMPANIES

Navigating the landscape of confusing hiring laws and regulations in the United States is essential for employers to ensure compliance and mitigate legal risks throughout the recruitment process. From anti-discrimination laws to regulations governing background checks and immigration, understanding these legal frameworks is crucial for fostering fair and equitable hiring practices. It will also keep you on the right side of the law.

Here is an overview of key regulations and laws governing hiring in the United States:

## 1. TITLE VII OF THE CIVIL RIGHTS ACT OF 1964

Title VII prohibits employment discrimination based on race, color, religion, sex, or national origin. This law applies to all aspects of the employment relationship, including hiring, promotion, compensation, and termination. Employers must ensure that their hiring practices are free from discrimination and bias, and they cannot make employment decisions based on protected characteristics.

## 2. AMERICANS WITH DISABILITIES ACT (ADA)

The ADA prohibits discrimination against qualified individuals with disabilities in all areas of public life, including employment. Employers must provide reasonable accommodations to qualified individuals with disabilities during the hiring process and throughout their employment. Additionally, employers cannot ask disability-related questions or require medical examinations before making a job offer.

## 3. AGE DISCRIMINATION IN EMPLOYMENT ACT (ADEA)

The ADEA prohibits discrimination against individuals who are 40 years of age or older. Employers cannot make employment decisions based on age, and they cannot specify age preferences or limitations in job postings unless age is a bona fide occupational qualification (BFOQ) for the position.

## 4. FAIR CREDIT REPORTING ACT (FCRA)

The FCRA regulates the use of consumer reports, including background checks, in the hiring process. Employers must obtain consent from candidates before conducting a background check and provide certain disclosures and notifications if adverse action is taken based on the results of the background check.

## 5. IMMIGRATION AND NATIONALITY ACT (INA)

The INA governs the employment of foreign nationals in the United States. Employers must verify the employment eligibility of all employees by completing Form I-9 and maintaining accurate records of employment verification. Additionally, employers must ensure compliance with visa requirements for foreign workers, including H-1B visas for skilled workers and L-1 visas for intracompany transferees.

## 6. FAMILY AND MEDICAL LEAVE ACT (FMLA)

The FMLA provides eligible employees with up to 12 weeks of unpaid, job-protected leave for certain family and medical reasons. Employers covered by the FMLA must inform employees of their rights under the law and provide leave for qualifying events, such as the birth or adoption of a child, a serious health condition, or caring for a family member with a serious health condition.

## 7. EQUAL EMPLOYMENT OPPORTUNITY COMMISSION (EEOC) GUIDELINES

The EEOC issues guidelines and regulations interpreting and enforcing federal employment discrimination laws, including Title VII, the ADA, and the ADEA. Employers must adhere to EEOC guidelines to ensure compliance with anti-discrimination laws and regulations.

## 8. STATE AND LOCAL LAWS

In addition to federal laws, employers must also comply with state and local laws governing hiring practices. These laws may impose additional requirements or protections for employees, such as prohibitions on salary history inquiries, ban-the-box laws restricting inquiries into criminal history, and requirements for paid sick leave or family leave.


## BEST PRACTICES FOR HIRING COMPLIANCE IN THE UNITED STATES

To ensure compliance with hiring laws and regulations in the United States, employers should:

- Develop written policies and procedures outlining the company's commitment to equal employment opportunity and non-discrimination.
- Provide regular training for hiring managers and human resources staff on anti-discrimination laws and best practices for hiring.

- Implement standardized hiring processes and criteria to minimize the risk of bias and discrimination and work to ensure that these practices are followed.
- Keep accurate records of hiring decisions, including job postings, applications, resumes, interview notes, and employment offers.
- Conduct regular disparate impact analyses for assessment results and hiring decisions.
- Consult legal counsel or expert HR professionals to ensure compliance with federal, state, and local laws and regulations.

By understanding and adhering to these laws and regulations, employers can create a fair and equitable hiring process that attracts and retains top talent while minimizing legal risks and liabilities.

For any questions about potential legal risks of your organization's hiring practices, please contact your employment lawyer.

127

# APPENDIX 2

# LEGAL COMPLIANCE FOR HIRING IN COUNTRIES OUTSIDE OF THE UNITED STATES

Navigating hiring laws and regulations for countries outside of the United States requires employers to understand the legal frameworks of individual countries and regions where they operate. From employment contracts to immigration requirements, each country has its own set of laws and regulations governing the hiring process. It is always prudent to check with local legal experts in employment laws and regulations to ensure that you stay within the bounds of rules and laws.

Here is an overview of key considerations for employers when hiring outside of the United States:

## 1. EMPLOYMENT CONTRACTS

In many countries, employment contracts are required by law and must outline the terms and conditions of employment, including salary, benefits, working hours, and termination procedures. Employers should familiarize themselves with local contract requirements and ensure compliance with applicable laws.

## 2. ANTI-DISCRIMINATION LAWS

Many countries have laws prohibiting discrimination in employment based on protected characteristics such as race, gender, age, religion, disability, or sexual orientation. Employers must comply with local anti-discrimination laws and ensure that their hiring practices are fair and equitable.

## 3. WORK AUTHORIZATION AND IMMIGRATION

Employers hiring foreign nationals must comply with local work authorization and immigration requirements. This may include obtaining work visas or permits for foreign employees, sponsoring visa applications, and adhering to quota restrictions or labor market tests imposed by immigration authorities.

## 4. MINIMUM WAGE AND BENEFITS

Countries may have minimum wage laws and regulations governing employee benefits such as paid time off, sick leave, maternity leave, and healthcare coverage. Employers must comply with local wage and benefit requirements and ensure that employees receive the minimum entitlements mandated by law.

## 5. PRIVACY AND DATA PROTECTION

Data protection laws regulate the collection, processing, and storage of personal information, including employee data. Employers must comply with local privacy and data protection laws when collecting and handling employee information during the hiring process.

## 6. EMPLOYMENT TAXES AND SOCIAL SECURITY CONTRIBUTIONS

Employers may be required to withhold and remit payroll taxes and social security contributions on behalf of employees. Tax rates and contribution requirements vary by country, and employers must ensure compliance with local tax laws and regulations.

## 7. EMPLOYMENT TERMINATION AND SEVERANCE

Countries have different laws and regulations governing employment termination, including notice periods, severance pay, and grounds for dismissal. Employers must adhere to local termination requirements and provide employees with any entitlements mandated by law.

## 8. COLLECTIVE BARGAINING AND UNIONIZATION

In countries where collective bargaining is prevalent, employers may be required to negotiate employment terms and conditions with labor unions or works councils. Employers must comply with collective bargaining agreements and engage in good-faith negotiations with employee representatives.


## BEST PRACTICES FOR HIRING COMPLIANCE OUTSIDE OF THE UNITED STATES

To ensure compliance with hiring laws and regulations outside of the United States, employers should:

- Conduct thorough research and seek legal advice on employment laws and regulations in each country where they operate.
- Develop standardized hiring processes and procedures that comply with local laws and regulations.
- Make sure that all decision-makers and hiring managers follow the set processes and procedures for hiring.
- Provide training for HR staff and hiring managers on international employment law compliance and best practices.

- Establish clear communication channels with local legal counsel, HR professionals, and government authorities to stay informed of changes in employment regulations.
- Maintain accurate records of hiring decisions, employment contracts, visa applications, and compliance documentation.

By understanding and adhering to the laws and regulations governing hiring outside of the United States, employers can navigate the complexities of international employment law and establish compliant and effective hiring practices in global markets.

For any questions about potential legal risks of your organization's hiring practices, please contact your employment lawyer.

# APPENDIX 3:

# ARTICLE – TESTIFYING AS AN EXPERT ON SKILLS-FIRST HIRING TO THE U.S. HOUSE OF REPRESENTATIVES

Mark A. Smith, Ph.D.

Mark Smith, Ph.D. provided expert testimony on June 22, 2023, before the House Committee on Education and the Workforce. As an organizational psychologist who has worked with many companies on applicant and employee testing, he was identified as a key expert in testing by committee members and staffers. He testified along with three other experts, including the chief economist at LinkedIn and the head of people at SAP.

"Every day, businesses miss out on talented people because their gifts, aptitude, and skills are more challenging to identify than a degree on a resume," Smith said in his opening statement.

"It's time we stop making the assumption that the only place to get skills is through college and getting a college degree," Smith told the committee in response to questions from one of the House members. "Organizations should worry more about the skills and less about where they came from."

In addition, Mark provided the committee with information on how employers can use skills assessments to evaluate a job applicant and broaden the pool of job applicants from which to hire.

He also pointed out that skills assessments are not the same as general cognitive ability tests. Skill tests that are properly developed and researched can be "unbiased and validated assessments that measure the critical knowledge and skills required to perform specific jobs," he testified. Specifically, he advocated for the use of job-relevant tests of knowledge and skills when evaluating job applicants.

---

*If you missed seeing him on CSPAN, you can see the video of his committee hearing "Competencies Over Degrees: Transitioning to a Skills-Based Economy" at this link:* https://www.youtube.com/live/Eia1ZrZyRHI?si=pw-3n7gjyKfcJzdZ

---

Here are some other key takeaways from the hearing:

*Skills-Based Hiring*: Employers are increasingly recognizing the value of assessing candidates based on their competencies and skills, rather than solely relying on formal degrees. This shift acknowledges that skills acquired through various pathways—such as work experience, certifications, and training—are equally valuable in today's dynamic job market.

*LinkedIn's Insights*: Dr. Karin Kimbrough, Chief Economist at LinkedIn, emphasized that when employers prioritize degrees, they miss out on a significant portion of the workforce. LinkedIn's extensive network data revealed that one in five job postings no longer requires a degree. Shifting to a skills-first approach can expand the pool of qualified workers by nearly 20 times.

*Technological Influence*: Technological advancements play a crucial role in reshaping the workforce landscape. Companies like SAP are at the forefront of skills-based practices. For instance, SAP assesses its employees' skills annually and provides personalized coaching. Regardless of their educational background, correlating skills to on-the-job performance enhances company achievement.

Mark A. Smith, Ph.D.

*Workforce Innovation and Opportunity Act (WIOA)*: To meet the demands of the modern economy, the committee discussed the importance of updating the legislative framework for workforce development. By dedicating resources to work-based skills development and simplifying employer participation, Congress can better equip companies to educate their employees effectively.

In summary, this hearing underscores the urgency of aligning our workforce system with the evolving job market. Competencies and skills are becoming the currency of employment, and adapting policies accordingly will benefit both employers and workers.

---

FOR MORE INFORMATION
https://edworkforce.house.gov/news/documentsingle.aspx?DocumentID=409345

135

# APPENDIX 4:

# GLOSSARY OF RECRUITING AND HIRING TERMS

**Age Discrimination in Employment Act (ADEA):**

A federal law in the United States prohibiting age discrimination against employees and job applicants aged 40 or older, ensuring fair treatment and opportunities in employment. This law was passed in 1967.

**Americans with Disabilities Act (ADA):**

A federal law protecting individuals with disabilities from discrimination in various areas, including employment, ensuring equal opportunities and reasonable accommodations. This law was passed in 1990.

**Applicant Tracking System (ATS):**

Software used by employers to streamline and manage the recruitment process, including job postings, candidate sourcing, resume screening, and applicant communication.

**Assessment Center:**

A centralized location (either real or virtual) where candidates undergo various assessment activities, such as tests, exercises, and simulations, to evaluate their suitability for a job role.

**Behavioral Assessment:**

A tool or method used to evaluate an individual's personality traits, behavioral tendencies, and competencies to assess their suitability for a job role.

**Candidate Experience:**

The perception and journey of job applicants throughout the recruitment process, encompassing interactions with the employer, communication, interview experiences, and overall satisfaction.

**Candidate Relationship Management (CRM):**

The strategic approach to managing and nurturing relationships with candidates throughout the recruitment process to enhance the candidate experience and improve talent acquisition outcomes.

**Civil Rights Act of 1964 (Title VII):**

A landmark federal law in the United States prohibiting discrimination based on race, color, religion, sex, or national origin in various aspects of employment, ensuring equal opportunities and treatment.

**Competencies**

The knowledge, skills, abilities, or other personal characteristics that it takes to do a job effectively. This can include a wide variety of traits, including personality-related and technical ones.

**Concurrent Validation:**

A method of validating selection procedures by demonstrating the relationship between test scores and job performance of current employees in the same position.

## Content-Based Validation:

Validation of selection procedures based on a thorough analysis of the job content and requirements to ensure alignment with job performance criteria. An important aspect of this approach is the linkage of test content and job tasks/duties.

## Culture Fit:

The alignment between a candidate's values, beliefs, and behaviors with those of the organization's culture.

## Disparate Impact:

Unintentional discrimination that occurs when an employment practice, policy, or criterion disproportionately affects a protected group, even if a standard approach is used and no discriminatory intent exists. This is also known as "adverse impact."

## Diversity, Equity, and Inclusion (DE&I):

Initiatives and practices aimed at creating a workforce that is diverse in terms of demographics, backgrounds, and perspectives, and inclusive of all individuals.

## Employer Brand:

The reputation, image, and perception of an organization as an employer, influencing its ability to attract, engage, and retain talent.

**Employee Referral Program:**

A structured program that incentivizes current employees to refer qualified candidates for open positions within their organization.

**Employer Value Proposition (EVP):**

The unique set of benefits and offerings that an employer promises to employees in exchange for their skills, capabilities, and commitment. The EVP is often created carefully as a marketing message would be created.

**Inbound Recruiting:**

A strategy focused on attracting candidates to an organization through content marketing, employer branding, and social media engagement.

**Job Aggregator:**

A website or platform that collects job listings from various sources across the internet and presents them to job seekers in one centralized location.

**Job Analysis:**

A systematic process of gathering, documenting, and analyzing information about a job's duties, responsibilities, tasks, and requirements to inform various HR functions, including recruitment, selection, and performance evaluation.

**Job Board:**

A website or online platform where employers can post job openings and candidates can search and apply for available positions.

**Job Description:**

A detailed document outlining the essential duties, responsibilities, qualifications, and expectations for a specific job role within an organization. Information from these documents is often used in job postings.

**Job Requisition:**

A formal request initiated by a hiring manager or department to fill a vacant position within an organization, specifying the job title, duties, requirements, and other relevant details.

**Key Performance Indicators (KPIs):**

Quantifiable measures used to evaluate the success and effectiveness of various aspects of the talent acquisition process.

**Onboarding:**

The process of integrating new employees into the organization, providing them with the necessary knowledge, skills, tools, and resources to become productive and engaged members of the team.

**Passive Candidate:**

An individual who is currently employed and not actively seeking a new job but may be open to new opportunities if presented with the right offer.

**Predictive Validation:**

A method of validating tests and other selection procedures by demonstrating the predictive relationship between test scores and future job performance of applicants.

**Psychometric Assessments:**

Standardized tests and tools used to measure individuals' cognitive abilities, personality traits, skills, and other psychological attributes relevant to job performance. The defining feature of these assessments is taking psychological factors and creating numerical scoring of them.

**Recruitment Automation:**

The use of technology, such as artificial intelligence and machine learning, to streamline and automate various aspects of the recruitment process.

**Recruitment Funnel:**

A visual representation of the stages that candidates progress through during the recruitment process, from awareness to hire.

**Recruitment Marketing:**

Strategies and tactics used to attract, engage, and nurture potential candidates by showcasing the employer brand, culture, opportunities, and value proposition.

**Recruitment Metrics:**

Quantitative measures used to evaluate the effectiveness of recruitment efforts, such as applicant-to-hire ratio, source of hire, and offer acceptance rate.

## Recruitment Process Outsourcing (RPO):

The practice of outsourcing some or all recruitment activities to an external service provider to improve efficiency and effectiveness.

## Role Play Assessments:

Evaluation method where candidates are asked to simulate specific work-related scenarios or situations to assess their skills, competencies, and behaviors. These role-play assessments are often used as part of a larger assessment center process.

## Selection Criteria:

The specific qualifications, skills, experience, and characteristics required for successful performance in a particular job role.

## Skills-First Hiring:

A recruitment approach that prioritizes assessing candidates based on their skills, competencies, and capabilities rather than solely focusing on their education or previous experience.

## Soft Skills:

Non-technical skills and personal attributes that enable individuals to effectively interact, communicate, collaborate, and adapt in various work environments.

**Sourcing:**

The proactive process of identifying, attracting, and engaging potential candidates through various channels such as job boards, social media, networking, and direct outreach.

**Structured Interviews:**

A standardized interview format where all candidates are asked a consistent set of predetermined questions, allowing for fair and objective assessment of their qualifications and fit for the job.

**Talent Acquisition:**

The process of identifying, attracting, and hiring skilled individuals to fulfill organizational needs and objectives. This is another term for "recruiting."

**Talent Acquisition Funnel:**

A visual representation of the recruitment process, depicting the stages through which candidates progress from sourcing to hire, including attraction, engagement, evaluation, and selection.

**Talent Management:**

The strategic process of attracting, developing, and retaining talented individuals to support organizational goals and objectives.

**Talent Mobility:**

The ability of employees to move within an organization, either horizontally or vertically, to pursue career advancement opportunities or address staffing needs.

**Talent Pool:**

A database or network of potential candidates who have been identified, assessed, and qualified for current or future job opportunities within an organization.

**Test Bias:**

Any systematic error or unfair advantage present in a selection test that results in different outcomes for individuals or groups based on irrelevant factors such as race, gender, or ethnicity.

**Test Proctoring**

The practice of monitoring individuals while they take a test or assessment to make sure that they are not cheating or attempting to copy the contents of the test. It can be done with live proctors or computerized (AI) proctors.

**Test Validation:**

The process of evaluating and documenting job relevance, effectiveness, fairness, and legality of selection tests or assessment procedures in predicting job performance.

**Uniform Guidelines on Employee Selection Procedures:**

United States federal guidelines providing principles and procedures for validating and using selection procedures to ensure fairness and minimize discrimination in employment practices.

**Workforce Analytics:**

The process of collecting, analyzing, and interpreting data related to workforce trends, performance, and demographics to inform decision-making and improve organizational effectiveness.


**Workforce Planning:**

The strategic process of forecasting future talent needs based on business objectives and developing plans to meet those needs.

##  Author Bio

**Mark Smith** is a respected HR consultant with a Ph.D. in organizational psychology and key experience in talent acquisition and assessments of both job applicants and employees. He spent five years at the Society for Human Resource Management after more than a decade as a consultant for HR departments in the private sector. Throughout his career, he has worked with all levels of employees (from hourly rate to executive levels) from different professions and industries. He has developed a reputation for creative and strategic approaches to assessment validation and research projects for all types of workplace issues. He currently works as an independent consultant and does regular work with Zennia Research.

In recent years, he presented expert testimony to the U.S. House Committee on Education and the Workforce about the use of assessments for skills-based hiring. He also worked with the Board on Human-Systems Integration for the National Academy of Science regarding the future of work.

He received his M.A. and Ph.D. degrees (I-O Psychology) from the University of South Florida and his B.A. (Psychology) from Hope College in Holland, Michigan. He grew up in Kalamazoo, Michigan.

You can find Mark on LinkedIn at: linkedin.com/in/mark-smith-ph-d-1776201a8. You can also email him directly at: msmitty63633@outlook.com.